A JOURNAL OF CONTEMPORARY WRITING

IRISH PAGES
DUILLÍ ÉIREANN

IRISH PAGES is a biannual journal (Spring-Summer, Autumn-Winter), edited in Belfast and publishing, in equal measure, writing from Ireland and overseas. It appears at the end of each six-month period.

Its policy is to publish poetry, short fiction, essays, creative non-fiction, memoir, essay reviews, nature-writing, translated work, literary journalism, and other autobiographical, historical, religious and scientific writing of literary distinction. There are no standard reviews or narrowly academic articles. Irish-language and Scots writing are published in the original, with English translations or glosses. IRISH PAGES is a non-partisan, non-sectarian, culturally ecumenical, and wholly independent journal. It endorses no political outlook or cultural tradition, and has no editorial position on the constitutional question. Its title refers to the island of Ireland in a purely apolitical and geographic sense, in the same manner of The Church of Ireland or the Irish Sea.

The sole criteria for inclusion in the journal are the distinction of the writing and the integrity of the individual voice. Equal editorial attention will be given to established, emergent and new writers.

The views expressed in IRISH PAGES are not necessarily those of the Editors. The journal is published by Irish Pages Ltd, a non-profit organization.

Submissions are welcome but must be accompanied by return postage or an international reply coupon. No self-addressed envelope is required. Reporting time is nine months. If work is accepted, a copy on disk may be requested.

Your subscription is essential to the independence and survival of the journal. Subscription rates are £16stg/€26/$45 for one year. Visit our website at www.irishpages.org for a subscription form or to order online. Credit cards are welcome.

IRISH PAGES
129 Ormeau Road
Belfast BT7 1SH

Advisory Board
Jonathan Allison
William Crawley
John Gray
Maureen Mackin
Bernard O'Donoghue
Daniel Tobin

Legal Advice: Kathy Mathews, Johnsons Law,
Belfast/Dublin/London

IRISH PAGES is designed by Alicia McAuley Publishing Services and set in 12/14.5 Monotype Perpetua. It is printed in Belfast by Nicholson & Bass.

This issue has been generously assisted by Foras na Gaeilge and the Arts Councils of Northern and Southern Ireland.

ISBN 978-0-9561046-3-2

Supported by
The National Lottery®
through the Arts Council of Northern Ireland

Foras na Gaeilge

Ulster-Scots Agency
Boord o Ulstèr-Scotch

IRISH PAGES

CHRIS AGEE, *Editor*

CATHAL Ó SEARCAIGH, *Irish Language Editor*

ANDREW PHILIP (Scotland) *and* STEPHEN DORNAN (Ulster),
Scots Language Editors

SEÁN MAC AINDREASA, *Managing Editor*

FIONA O'HEA, *Assistant Managing Editor*

AONGHAS MACLEÒID *and* JACOB AGEE, *Editorial Assistants*

EDITED IN BELFAST
VOLUME 8, NUMBER 2

IRISH PAGES
DUILLÍ ÉIREANN

VOLUME 8, NUMBER 2

CONTENTS

Heaney

IN MEMORIAM SEAMUS HEANEY
A Suite of Obituaries

The Patrons of This Issue

MARIE HEANEY

&

DONNELL and ALISON DEENY

—

FRIENDS OF IRISH PAGES

—

The next issue of Irish Pages, *"After Heaney" (Vol 9, No 1), will focus on the poet's creative, critical and cultural legacy.*

Seamus Heaney: Study
By Jeffrey Morgan
2008

FOUR POEMS

Seamus Heaney

A FOUND POEM

Like everybody else, I bowed my head
during the consecration of the bread and wine,
lifted my eyes to the raised host and raised chalice,
believed (whatever it means) that a change occurred.
I went to the altar rails and received the mystery
on my tongue, returned to my place, shut my eyes fast, made
an act of thanksgiving, opened my eyes and felt
time starting up again.
There was never a scene
when I had it out with myself or with an other.
The loss of faith occurred off stage. Yet I cannot
disrespect words like "thanksgiving" or "host"
or even "communion wafer". They have an undying
pallor and draw, like well water far down.

BILL COLE'S LPs

As Dante when he entered Purgatory
Was greeted by Casella, and the song
Casella sang wakened a memory

Of loves they'd known and music and many a long
Long afternoon of wine and poetry,
So I, when I heard, that William Cole had gone

To meet the shades, imagined him and me
Meeting again in an earthly paradise –
Not in his old off-Broadway Flat 6b,

His book grotto, his cove of revery,
Of trysts daydreamt while we replayed the LPs –
But where we'd never meet, in Co Derry,

On the banks of the Moyola, and his voice
Rising up there in an Irish tenor brogue
McCormack might have envied, or James Joyce,

Or Moore in Avoca, by Avonmore and Beg.
River rhyming, over-brimming, young
At heart, and younger song by song.

BANKS OF A CANAL
Gustave Caillebotte, circa *1872*

Say "canal" and there's that final vowel
Towing silence with it, slowing time
To a walking pace, a path, a whitewashed gleam
Of dwellings at the skyline. World stands still.
The stunted concrete mocks the classical.
Water says, "My place here is in dream,
In quiet good standing. Like a sleeping stream,
Come rain or sullen shine I'm peaceable."
Stretched to the horizon, placid ploughland,
The sky not truly bright or overcast:
I know that clay, the damp and dirt of it,
The coolth along the bank, the grassy zest
Of verges, the path not narrow but still straight
Where soul could mind itself or stray beyond.

IN A FIELD

And there I was in the middle of a field,
The furrows once called "scores" still with their gloss,
The tractor with its hoisted plough just gone

Snarling at an unexpected speed
Out on the road. Last of the jobs,
The windings had been ploughed, furrows turned

Three ply or four round each of the four sides
Of the breathing land, to mark it off
And out. Within that boundary now

Step the fleshy earth and follow
The long healed footprints of one who arrived
From nowhere, unfamiliar and de-mobbed,

In buttoned khaki and buffed army boots,
Bruising the turned-up acres of our back field
To stumble from the windings' magic ring

And take me by a hand to lead me back
Through the same old gate into the yard
Where everyone has suddenly appeared,

All standing waiting.

The above four poems are uncollected. "A Found Poem" was published in an American volume, The God Factor: Inside the Spiritual Lives of Public People *(Farrar, Straus & Giroux), edited by the journalist Cathleen Flasani, and is a poetic recension of a passage that later appears in* Stepping Stones: Interviews with Seamus Heaney, *by Dennis O'Driscoll (Faber, 2009). "Bill Coles LPs" is a revised version of "In Memory of Bill Coles" (which was published in* The Brooklyn Rail *in 2001), and subsequently appeared in* The Clifden Anthology *and* The Irish Times *on the anniversary of Heaney's death. "Banks of a Canal" appeared posthumously in* Lines of Vision: Irish Writers on Art, *edited by Janet McLean (Thames & Hudson, 2014). "In a Field" was published in* 1914: Poetry Remembers *(Faber) in late 2013. They are published courtesy of the copyright Estate of Seamus Heaney.*

Seamus Heaney was awarded the Nobel Prize for Literature in 1995. His twelfth collection of poems, Human Chain *(Faber), was published in 2010. He died in Blackrock Clinic, Dublin, at 7.30 am on 30 August 2013 and is buried in the family plot in Bellaghy Cemetery, Bellaghy, Co Derry. He is survived by his wife, Marie; his children, Michael, Catherine Ann and Christopher; and his granddaughters, Aoibheann and Anna Rose Heaney.*

SECOND THOUGHTS & CODA

—

Helen Vendler

Tell the truth. Do not be afraid.

—

SECOND THOUGHTS

Seamus Heaney, the most famous English-language poet of his era, and (as was often said) the greatest Irish poet since W.B. Yeats, was in 1995 awarded the Nobel Prize "for works of lyrical beauty and ethical depth, which exalt everyday miracles and the living past." His public readings attracted large appreciative audiences, not only in Ireland and Great Britain and the United States but also throughout Europe. Heaney, although best known for his work as a poet, was also a prose writer of vigor and eloquence. He also ventured into the adaptation of Sophoclean tragedy when, in conjunction with the Field Day Theatre, he produced English "versions" (as he preferred to characterize them) of *Philoctetes* (under the title *The Cure at Troy*) and *Antigone* (under the title *The Burial at Thebes*). Heaney was also a notable translator, not only of the Anglo-Saxon epic *Beowulf* but also (in "version" form) of the anonymous Middle-Irish narrative *Buile Suibhne* (rendered as *Sweeney Astray*), and of the Middle-Scots *The Testament of Cresseid* & *Seven Fables* of Robert Henryson. Scattered in various volumes are translations of excerpts from Virgil, Ovid, and other poets, and at the time of Heaney's death a limited edition of his translation of Book VI of *The Aeneid* was in preparation. A book-length interview by Dennis O'Driscoll, published in 2008 as *Stepping Stones*, is the fullest rendering of Heaney's own view of his life and work.

Heaney, born in Castledawson, County Derry, Northern Ireland, grew up as the first child of nine born to Patrick Heaney, a cattle-dealer, and his wife Margaret. Patrick's sister Mary shared the house, and Heaney's first memory (revealed in "Mossbawn") was of his aunt Mary's making and baking scones: "And here is love / like a tinsmith's scoop / sunk past its gleam / in the meal-bin." After elementary school in Anahorish, Heaney won a scholarship enabling him to become a boarder at the Catholic St

Columb's School in Derry, a period vividly recalled in the sequence "Alphabets", in which Heaney traces his schooling in English, Latin, and Irish, a process by which the world is widened beyond his rural upbringing. During Heaney's time at St Columb's, his four-year-old brother Christopher was killed in a road accident: the tragedy is described in one of Heaney's most famous poems, "Mid-Term Break".

It was at Queen's University, Belfast, that Heaney began to write poems under the pen-name "Incertus": "I went disguised in it, ... tagging it under my efforts like a damp fuse. Uncertain." Heaney left Queen's in 1964 with a first in English and, after a year at St Joseph's teacher-training college, was for a year an intermediate-school teacher before being appointed to the staff at St Joseph's. At this time, he met the English critic and poet Philip Hobsbaum, who formed in Dublin (as he had in London previously) a group of young poets who met regularly to read and critique each other's work. Hobsbaum forwarded Heaney's work to London, where it was seen by Karl Miller, Editor of *The New Statesman*, who in 1964 published three poems, including the well-known poem of vocation, "Digging": "Between my finger and my thumb / The squat pen rests. / I'll dig with it." In 1965, Faber published Heaney's first volume of poems, *Death of a Naturalist*, which was followed by eleven more collections. The most substantial collected edition, *Opened Ground: Poems 1966–1996*, was, by the time of Heaney's death in 2013, missing poems from the volumes published in 2001 (*Electric Light*), 2006 (*District and Circle*) and 2010 (*Human Chain*). In 2009, to celebrate Heaney's seventieth birthday, Faber brought out a collection of CDs on which Heaney recorded all his published poems to that point, but no *Complete Poems* was ever issued. A bibliography of Heaney's work by Rand Brandes was published in 2008.

In 1965, Heaney married Marie Devlin, a teacher and writer; three children, Michael, Christopher, and Catherine, were born of the marriage. In 1966, Heaney became a Lecturer at Queen's University, Belfast, and in 1970, he accepted an offer to be a Visiting Lecturer at the University of California, Berkeley, returning to Queen's in 1971. The California venture introduced Heaney to the United States and its contemporary poets, both native and foreign; Czeslaw Miłosz, the great Polish poet, was teaching at Berkeley and became, for Heaney, an example of the life of poetry lived at the highest level (Heaney was later to write a poem about Miłosz entitled "The Master"). In California, Heaney wrote the remarkable poems in *Wintering Out* (1972), in which his social canvas began to extend itself in

13

several directions. Whereas in his first two books he had been chiefly occupied with his country childhood and its "calendar customs", he now began to write about social injustice, choosing (in a decision unusual in a man of his generation) to expose the cruelty of Irish society toward women who had borne children out of wedlock. In "Limbo", a frightened young mother drowns her baby rather than risk discovery; in "Bye-Child", an "illegitimate" child, kept hidden alone in a dark hen-house and fed surreptitiously by his mother, is at last freed; he lacks the capacity of speech. The social canvas extends to a candid picture of marital smouldering in "Summer Home", and, further afield, the poet reaches out to the first of the "bog bodies" described by P.V. Glob in *The Bog People*. "The Tollund Man", found strangled, his body preserved by the tannin in the bog, seems to the poet analogous to the murdered contemporary bodies of Northern Ireland, Revolted by the killing in his own country, the poet imagines visiting the Jutland of the bog bodies: "Out there in Jutland / In the old man-killing parishes / I will feel lost, / Unhappy and at home."

After Heaney's return to Queen's in 1972, the political "Troubles" in Northern Ireland, which had increased in intensity and danger since the sixties, determined the move of the poet and his family to the Republic of Ireland, where they lived south of Dublin in Glanmore, County Wicklow, in a cottage that had served as the gatekeeper's lodge of the Synge estate. Heaney had given up his lectureship at Queen's, and the family lived frugally for four years on his freelance work and Marie's income as an elementary-school teacher. It was at Glanmore that Heaney wrote his most famous volume, *North* (1975), which became (and remains) a site of controversy. In it, Heaney reflected the violence erupting in the North as the political and economic tensions between the dominant Protestant Unionists and the Catholic minority (suffering discrimination in employment and education) came to a head. Placing "the Troubles" in a larger geographical and historical context, Heaney imagined the long history of killing, of "neighborly murder", in the northern regions of Europe; he recalled as well the Viking invasions and the savage execution of enemies: such cruelty was symbolized by the torture of an adulterous medieval woman whose body was found in an Irish bog. In such famous poems as "Bog Queen" and "Punishment", Heaney indicts both himself and his culture.

After four years in Glanmore, Heaney moved to Dublin and accepted a lectureship at Carysfort College (a teaching college), where he served as head of department, a task leaving him little time for writing. He was invited to Harvard for a visiting appointment, arriving in 1981, and was then appointed to the tenured Boylston Professorship of Rhetoric and Oratory, committing himself to teaching at Harvard for one semester every year (and honoring the commitment even in the year he won the Nobel). His wife Marie, facing single motherhood of three children for three months a year, did not flinch, but said to me, "All I want is for Seamus to be able to write his poems." Backed by her support, Heaney embarked on a happy and successful career at Harvard, where he taught both Creative Writing and Contemporary Irish Poetry (a course which omitted his own work). He concluded his formal teaching at Harvard in 1997, but from 1998 to 2006 visited for a few weeks each year as the Emerson Poet in Residence. In 1989, while at Harvard, he was elected to the five-year non-resident position of Professor of Poetry at Oxford, delivering three lectures yearly, some of which were collected under the title *The Redress of Poetry* (1995). *Finders Keepers: Selected Prose 1971–2001* gives a broad overview of his prose works – autobiographical, biographical, and literary. His critical opinions were forthright, but courteously offered. He wrote widely on Irish, English, Welsh, and Scottish authors, but the years in the United States had also introduced him to the work of the postwar American poets, among whom he found Elizabeth Bishop especially sympathetic. He had of course known the work of Eliot and Pound and Frost from his youth, and once, in conversation with me, surprisingly named Frost as his favorite poet. Heaney's prose brought new energy to contemporary critical writing about poetry: brilliantly accurate, it was voiced in a tone of colloquial engagement with his audience. It assumed that poetry was an indispensable part of any culture, serving to bring current concerns to the fore but also to recreate, in free play, the fabric of language.

In *North*, Heaney had continued to use the "thin" stanza he had explored in his second and third volumes, deriving it from slender forms of poetry in the Irish language, and contrasting it, in later remarks, with the broad pentameters of Wordsworth and Keats and Hopkins, poets that had first inspired him. With increasing frequency, Heaney prolongs his subject-matter by composing sequences, gathering a series of short poems under a single title. These, beginning with the seven-member "A Lough Neagh Sequence" in Heaney's second volume, *Door into the Dark*, take on more and more weight over time until, in 1984, the poet publishes the 12-member autobiographical sequence "Station Island" (the title poem for his sixth volume of verse). In another autobiographical sequence, "Sweeney Redivivus", Heaney exposes himself, under the guise of Sweeney (the bird-hero of *Sweeney Astray*) to ironic questioning of his own history. He has now exhausted, as a primary subject, the earlier narratives of his childhood life and its religious observance; he has left behind the North and its troubles; he has taken a period of seclusion in Glanmore (recorded in his 1979 seventh volume, *Field Work*), and he now finds himself, in "On the Road" — the closing poem of "Sweeney Redivivus" — seeking a new source of poetry. Leaving Christianity behind, he migrates (still in the bird-persona of Sweeney) down to the "deepest chamber" of a prehistoric cave, finding there, incised in the rock, "a drinking deer" with its "nostril flared // at a dried up source." He resolves to wait there "until the long dumbfounded / spirit broke cover / to raise a dust / in the font of exhaustion."

The new energy that seemed unattainable in "On the Road" arose from an unlikely source: a Polish poet, Czeslaw Miłosz, and his contemporaries. These poets, writing under censorship, often turned to allegory as a vehicle of moral meditation, and *The Haw Lantern* (1987), Heaney's eighth volume, betrays their influence in such allegorical poems as "From the Republic of Conscience", "From the Frontier of Writing", "From the Canton of Expectation", and "The Mud Vision."

The Haw Lantern's sequence "Clearances", an elegy for the poet's mother, represents a new venture in Heaney's poetry, as his next volume *Seeing Things* (1991) takes as its subject invisible things. The invisibles include the dead, who remain only as absences; the interior (but invisible) sensings and mountings of which Wordsworth spoke, the abstract geometrical forms living in the architectural space of the mind; the measures of mathematics, perceived even when merely imagined. In "Song", a poem from the earlier Glanmore period, Heaney had described himself as a poet of the everyday: "There are the mud-flowers of dialect / And the immortelles of perfect pitch / And that moment when the bird sings very close / To the music of what happens." Now, in *Seeing Things*, Heaney resolves to leave poetry that is "Sluggish in the doldrums of what happens" and to turn to those intellectual and emotional invisibles that contend against a material concept of the real.

Heaney's father had died in 1986, completing the erasure of the poet's childhood experience (elegized in "Clearances" as "a space / utterly empty, utterly a source"). Patrick Heaney's death lies under Heaney's longest sequence, "Squarings", included in *Seeing Things*. This is a series of 48 12-line poems, each consisting of 4 broad-lined tercets, making a square shape on the page. The sequence itself is subdivided into 4 groups of 12 poems, each representing a perfect square: 12 (lines per poem) by 12 (poems). In the tenth poem, as the poet contemplates a flooded quarry, he isolates his theme: the irreconcilable confrontation of the invisible and the material. "Ultimate // Fathomableness, ultimate / Stony up-againstness: could you reconcile / What was diaphanous there with what was massive?" Heaney confronts the insufficiencies of both art and nature to human existence: "How habitable is perfected form? / And how inhabited the windy light?"

The Spirit Level (1996) praises stoic endurance in the person of the poet's brother Hugh, who, living among the armed outbreaks in the North, kept the family farm ("Keeping Going"). But against that patience Heaney sets the corruption of both kingship and marriage in Aeschylus's *Agamemnon*. It was only after the subsidence of the quarter-century of conflict in Northern Ireland that Heaney could allow his language a violence corresponding to the political violence he had seen and felt. In the bitter poems comprising "Mycenae Lookout", Heaney takes on the persona of the Watchman, who observes, at the return of Agamemnon and his sexual captive Cassandra from Troy, the obscene fantasies of the crowd, followed by the murder of both Agamemnon and Cassandra by Clytemnestra and her lover Aegisthus. The sequence concludes with a fatalistic view of the perpetual persistence of aggression, of "besieger and besieged", but its most memorable lines are those reporting terror and slaughter. And although *The Spirit Level* closes with the Northern Irish ceasefire and a "postscript" of light, water, and swans in County Clare, the inhumanity of the Troubles is not entirely routed. As the poet realizes the metamorphoses of self over time, he describes his identity, so solid in childhood, as a phenomenon in perpetual flux: "You are neither here nor there, / A hurry through which known and strange things pass."

Heaney's next two volumes, *Electric Light* (2001) and *District and Circle* (2006), continued in an elegiac atmosphere, with moving vignettes of past and present; *District and Circle* contained "Anything Can Happen", Heaney's poem on the 2001 destruction of the Twin Towers (adapted from an Horatian ode in which human destiny is governed not by a benign Providence but by a malign Fate. A new note was struck in *Human Chain* (2010), where poems written in the wake of Heaney's 2006 stroke celebrated, with marked tenderness, family and friends, "the ones who have known him all along." The volume culminates in a long autobiographical sequence called "Route 110" in which Heaney draws parallels between episodes in his own life and events in *The Aeneid*, especially Aeneas's sojourn in the underworld and his meeting there with the ghosts of his father and of Dido.

In 2013, Heaney was hospitalized in Dublin for treatment of an aneurysm. After his departure for the operating room, Marie Heaney, to her sudden surprise, received on her cellphone a text sent by Seamus as he awaited the operation. The text included the Latin "*Noli timere*", "Do not be afraid": Heaney was quoting from his own poem "The Master", in which the neophyte seeking knowledge finds, after an arduous climb to the tower of the Master, "just the old rules / we all had inscribed on our slates ... // *Tell the truth. Do not be afraid.*" Heaney died just before the operation was to begin, instantly and with his faculties intact.

Heaney's work was awarded numerous prizes in Ireland, England, the United States, and Europe, from his first book (which won both the Gregory Award and the Geoffrey Faber Prize) to his last (which won the Forward Poetry Prize for Best Collection), with the 1995 Nobel (and many others) coming in between. His poetry attracted a large readership, beginning with those in Ireland who remembered rural childhoods and customs resembling his own, and widening over time to the world-audiences that heard his unaffected and moving readings or who knew the poems in English or in translation. The poetry was reassuring in its compassion and understanding of human sadness, hostility, and loss; it was nostalgic in its reconstruction of a vanished pre-industrial Ireland; it was honest in refusing political ideology and political propaganda; it was humane in its candid depictions of married dissension and married love; and (after a long period of holding back) it allowed itself an outburst of rage at human cruelty and the indifference of fate. Like its author, the work was at home in allusion and etymology, but both were so deftly touched on that they could glide easily into mind or recollection. Heaney's wonderfully modulated rhythms could be angular or lulling, martial or dance-like, melodic or staccato; and his alert revisions of the subgenres of Western lyric – the epithalamion, the christening-poem, the pastoral, the elegy, the erotic poem, the *hommage*, the journey poem, the eclogue, the hagiography – have yet to be described fully. His work gave courage to other poets who, remaining within the tradition, could dare, as he did, to alter it by their individual talent.

In person, Heaney was welcoming, generous, and witty; his household in Dublin was the site of warm welcome to visitors from all over the world.

His humor arrived in a quip or in repartee rather than in any bravura display. His natural posture was a modest one, from his young days onward, and he remained firmly grounded in the body that never forgot the muscular life of spades and pitchforks. He had a sense of duty that he took only too seriously; he could not dismiss any genuine inquiry or any obligation to family and friends, to whom he was sturdily loyal. He was not sentimental, although he was brimming with sentiment; he gave the appalling its due. His elegy for his sister Ann, who died of cancer, included the full hospital ghastliness of the fright in her face, just as his poem about washing his dying father included his own revulsion from the slack skin of the aged flesh. His high intelligence compelled, throughout his work, second thoughts that queried his first ones; as he said himself in "Terminus", "Is it any wonder when I thought / I would have second thoughts?" Like Chekhov writing about the prison on Sakhalin, he strove – in an atmosphere riddled with dogma, declaration, and threat – "To try for the right tone – not tract, not thesis."

———

CODA

Seamus Heaney's funeral in Dublin was televized live, marking an event that occupied the front pages in Ireland for several days. In his eulogy of the poet, Paul Muldoon told the story of being asked at customs, on his arrival for the funeral, what he did for a living; when he replied that he taught poetry, the customs officer said, "You must be devastated." No need to say why: the loss of the poet was felt everywhere. He had visited schools and given readings in almost every corner of the country, often for nothing; thousands of people had seen him on television, or had read of the Nobel Prize. The bleak fact that there would be no next volume of his poetry was a grief to his readers, but even those who knew his work best were mourning the man as much as the poet.

Seamus established an immediate intimacy even with strangers. The eldest of nine children, he could be anyone's older brother. A quick understanding and quiet help arose naturally in him. He had a ready humor: I once took a cab in Cambridge a day after Seamus's departure to Oxford, and the driver said: "I had a very witty man in the cab yesterday." You couldn't meet Seamus without seeing how unusual he was in perception and how rapidly he took in another person. At Harvard, he and I had both taught an exceptionally gifted student who died young. His student friends asked me if perhaps Seamus could send some words to be read at the memorial service. I left the message for Seamus in Dublin, and in a few hours found a return message with a tender paragraph about the student. The kindness was typical; but what arrested me, when I heard that description on my voice mail, was its uncanny accuracy. He had taught the student several years earlier, but it was as though he could lift from memory a photographic scan of the student and, by a sort of alchemy, "read it off" into factual and touching statement. I realized then that Seamus "scanned" people in a clairvoyant way, realizing their faculties of mind and temperament instantly and deeply.

It was that scanning, putting feeling into words, which distinguished Seamus's portraits of human beings. In his poem "Mid-Term Break" (recalling, years later, the death of his four-year-old brother, hit by a car), he is an adolescent sitting at the wake next to his mother, who "coughed out angry tearless sighs." The phrase gives me, by its convincing oddity, the absolute joy that art provides. "Cough": an uncontrollable spasm of the throat; "anger": an outward-going fierce resentment; "tearless": a violent suppression of the body's natural response; "sigh": a declining volume of breath, yes, but when coupled with "angry" a self-propelling protesting ungovernable exhalation, rising upward again as soon as it dies away. Around the unforgettable past scan of his mother's anguished voicelessness, words – "cough", "anger", "tearless", "sigh" – begin to cluster in the poet's mind, translating the buried scan into language. Heaney's particular mosaic of words preserves the unique, complex, and unrepeatable contour of human emotion: "what we felt at what we saw", as Stevens put it. Such a run of words tells the human tale in the way it is lived: moment by moment. Forgettable poems cannot delineate the uniqueness of the moment: their language is half cliché, ruining itself as it goes.

And so, volume by volume, decade by decade, Heaney translated feelings in resonant word-clusters. For "the Troubles" in Northern Ireland: "neighbourly murders." For early marriage: "the lovely and painful / Covenants of flesh ... / The respite in our dewy dreaming faces." For expressing his chosen but unnatural distance from his native North when he moved to the Republic: "I am neither internee nor informer; / an inner émigré." After his mother's death: "A soul ramifying and forever / Silent, beyond silence listened for." For the destruction of the Twin Towers: "Anything can happen." And in the course of a long career, around the clusters there clustered more clusters, until a constellation, and then in time a galaxy, shone from the assembled poems, making up what we call a poet's style.

Heaney's own style went through many changes while remaining recognizable across time. Brought up a Catholic, he was no longer a believer as an adult, but he also remarked that one cannot forget the culture in which one was raised. He attended no church, but by his own wish was buried at a Catholic Mass: there is no other way to bury someone from the Catholic tradition in Ireland. The readings reflected the poet's multiple debts to foundational texts: the Hebrew Bible ("Let us now praise famous men", "a time to be born and a time to die", the twenty-third psalm); and the New Testament ("the greatest of these is charity"). The Gospel of the day included Jesus's reassurances concerning the fall of the sparrow and the lilies of the field. The homilist of the removal ceremony the night before had invoked Irish legend, reading part of Seamus's poem on St Kevin and the blackbird, a parable of saintly human kindness. The funeral music (except for the organ of the liturgy) was provided by Liam O'Flynn's uillean pipes, playing minor-key melodies of Irish lament. A solo cello at the end played Brahms's lullaby. Although the sorry English of the new Biblical translation of "The Lord is My Shepherd" marred the reading of that psalm, the other Biblical texts were read in the traditional English of the Douay Bible, keeping the dignity of language in view. Peter Fallon read Heaney's beautiful poem "The Given Note", about a violinist composing an air: it concerns the aspect of art that seems not made but rather bestowed "out of the night":

> So whether he calls it spirit music
> Or not, I don't care. He took it
> Out of wind off mid-Atlantic.

> Still, he maintains, from nowhere.
> It comes off the bow gravely,
> Rephrases itself into the air.

Paul Muldoon gave a heartfelt account of the man and the poetry; Michael Heaney ended the ceremony with an offering of thanks to all mourners on the part of the family, and a eulogy of Seamus as husband and father.

In short, the readings were as mixed as Heaney himself, and the chosen music was secular (not liturgical or hymnic), played on two instruments —

one from the folk tradition and one from the classical orchestra. It was a sober funeral, with the family – Marie Heaney, Michael, Catherine, and Christopher – in the first row of the pews, patiently shaking hands with hundreds of mourners at the end of the service. A public funeral, with the President and the Taoiseach in attendance, and the video cameras everywhere. A private funeral, with Heaney's two sons and two of his brothers among the pallbearers. An austere funeral, with a single spray of white flowers on the coffin.

These articles appeared, respectively, in the American Philosophical Society Bulletin *and* The New Republic *shortly after Heaney's death.*

One of the foremost poetry scholars and critics in the Anglophone world, Helen Vender is A. Kingsley Porter Professor at Harvard University. She is the author of 21 works of scholarship, including Seamus Heaney *(Harper Collins, 1998) and, most recently,* Dickinson: Selected Poems and Commentaries *(Harvard University Press, 2010). She was a close friend and colleague of Seamus Heaney for many years.*

THRENODY FOR SEAMUS

Kerry Hardie

I've taken a sick dog to the vet and we're waiting.
A man comes in, youngish, his face full of weather,
asking for syringes and milk powder –
brand names I don't know, stuff for lambs.
I sit soothing the dog, watching Fiona
getting things off the shelves, filling brown paper bags,
then send him off, his arms full.
That man's asleep on his feet, I say, and she laughs.
It's the time of year –
February – thin and hard and sharpened with rain,
a few snowdrops up, sticking close to the ground,
the river run wild, drowning fences, pulling trees
down into itself, and for some reason I start thinking
about where my life's gone – how it's slipping through my fingers
like the little bright fish in the handful of water
I dip for in August when this same river
has shallows
and pooled light
and banks blowsy with meadowsweet and agrimony,
all tumbled and trailed down into the water,
and the swallows make glitters of light taking flies,
and swimsuits hang on farm washing lines,
and the young girls stroll their stuff in pairs,
and the old women sit in the doorways, their stockings
rolled into soft latex doughnuts around their ankles,
and the land breathes and eases and stretches –
Not the usual time of year to go dying.

Life's like the fish, just a wriggle of light
that slips through your fingers
and slides away off down the river,
in February or May or even August.
And it's colder here without you.
And Dennis, already gone –

Kerry Hardie was born in Singapore in 1951 and grew up in Co Down. She is the author of six collections of poems, most recently The Ash and the Oak and the Wild Cherry Tree *(The Gallery Press, 2012) and two novels,* Hannie Bennett's Winter Marriage *and* The Bird Woman *(Harper Collins, 2000 and 2006). She is a member of Aosdána, and lives in Milltown, Co Kilkenny.*

PORTFOLIO

Bobbie Hanvey

Seamus Justin Heaney
13 April 1939–30 August 2013

At home.
1996

Bobbie Hanvey (b. 1945) is a photographer, writer, journalist and broadcaster from Brookeborough, Co Fermanagh. In the 1960s, he worked as a psychiatric nurse in Co Down, and his novel, The Mental *(Wonderland Press, 2002), offers a rare view of everyday life in 1950s Fermanagh and at the Downshire Mental Hospital. He has also hosted a popular programme, "The Ramblin' Man", on Northern Ireland's Downtown Radio, for the past 28 years.*

    Hanvey is one of Ireland's leading photographers. For the past four decades he has chronicled the people and life in the North of Ireland. He is the author of two acclaimed books of photographs, Merely Players: Portraits from Northern Ireland, *and* Last Days of the R.U.C., First Days of the P.S.N.I. *He lives in Downpatrick, Co Down.*

In a Bellaghy bog,
with the hat, overcoat and walking stick of his father.
1985

Amid turfstacks, in a Bellaghy bog.
1985

With extended family members.
1980s

With daughter Catherine Ann, sons Michael and Christopher,
and wife Marie.
1979

Seamus's father, Patrick; sister, Anne; and mother, Margaret.
1970s

Anne Heaney (Seamus's sister).
1970s

With guests, at a party in his Dublin home.
1979

With a group of musicians (back row: Arty McGlynn, Gene Stewart, Paul Brady, Tommy Sands and Nollaig Casey), and the painter T.P. Flannagan (centre front).
1989

Marie Heaney (Seamus's wife).
1996

1990s

1988

At Sandymount Pier, Dublin.
1996

Walking on Sandymount Pier, Dublin.
1996

1996

Speaking at the opening of Bellaghy Bawn, Bellaghy, Co Derry.
1996

At the opening of Bellagy Bawn, signing a book for Rebecca Deeny,
with her father Donnell.
1996

At the new building of his old primary school.
1996

1990s

In his study.
2000s

1990s

Seamus's cortège, Bellaghy Cemetery,
Bellaghy, Co Derry.
2 September 2013

Seamus's coffin, carried by sons Michael and Christopher,
and brothers Hugh and Daniel.
2 September 2013

Seamus's family at the graveside,
with thurible-smoke in the foreground.
2 September 2013

PORTFOLIO

is generously supported by Nicholson & Bass Ltd, Belfast.

DEAR AFTERLIFE

Michael Coady

i.m. *Dennis O'Driscoll, who died Christmas Eve 2012*

Dennis, poet, man of letters,
I've faith and hope that you and I
might still enjoy between the lines
some kind of intercom,
never mind that you
are destined now to go on
singing dumb.

And so that's where I'm coming from
with this account of your send-off —
assuming you can link
from that other side
to which you were so abruptly
snatched from Naas on Christmas Eve

around the very time that I
was following my wife
into a Kilkenny shop
where, while she felt her way
through racks of resale clothes,
I picked up for a song
three symphonies of Haydn
and a hardbound translation of
Rousseau's *Confessions*.

How strange — yet not strange at all
since life was in full swing —
that on that afternoon
while I played my own Santa Claus
in High Street, Kilkenny,
you were headed into mystery

of ultimate lift-off from
the general hospital of Nás na Rí,
leaving Julie beside herself
in untold shock and grief amid
tinsel, carols, Christmas trees
that eve of the Nativity.

Remember then, after the feast,
on the last day of the year
we walked you through the town,
a dozen or so bards to hand
forming an honour guard's embrace
both sides of the hearse
under insinuating rain.

Back there in the church
we'd shared a deep communion
of love and loss (how good it was
to chant *Kyrie Eleison*). Whatever else,
we recognise the proper weight of death —
its drop to final deep beyond coastline
and continental shelf.

Standing there to speak for you, Seamus, your friend
the tousle-headed kern, *saoi*
of Derry fields and byres and sheughs
as well as halls and towers of Academe.
Could he have had an inkling
of the shadow at his shoulder,
how, in mere months to come
he too would follow on the path
of no return?

See us shuffle towards the graveyard
on that New Year's Eve. You may
have been surprised to note
(in cars, shop doorways or on footpaths)
how many men and women pause
to bless themselves as we pass by.
I salute their decency,
recalling words of Eudora Welty:
Every feeling waits upon its gesture.

A sign up front insists GET IN LANE —
something you could have devised
to put the wind up in us
no matter how we try to veer today
tomorrow or next year —

and you're still showing us the score
when towards the edge of town
the hearse driver signals a left turn
into St Corban's place of graves
where, to the side, another sign
reads LOW HEADROOM.

At this point the honour guard
slightly ahead, takes a wrong turn
and briefly loses contact
with the whole cortège.
But there it is upon another path
and with as much aplomb
as can be faked the bards accelerate,
short-cut across the dead,
coming in first at the finish line
of the open grave until
you and the rest arrive.

Final rituals are seen to and intoned,
we chant *Salve Regina*
and one way or another
you are home.

I share this reportage with you
and possible posterity
because at heart we're story-tellers
to one another in this world,
including in our tellings those
no longer visible within
the firelit circle of the living.

The grave-diggers stand by
waiting to close earth's open
mouth again and tidy up.
Theirs is a job that gets
into the pores, and to the core.
They'll spruce up later on,
head out on the town
to bid farewell to the old year
and see the new one in.

Nothing for it then but leave you there
and drift away, by-passing the signs
for *get in lane* and *low headroom*
this darkening afternoon.
In Lawlors Hotel hot whiskeys
are the order of the day
and there before us is a gathering
of army officers in dress uniform,
their swords unbuckled by the fire.

Has there been some kind of *coup d'état*
at the Curragh while we were off guard?

Nothing so dramatic, Dennis:
no sooner were you carried from the church
than an army wedding party
was warming up to enter in. This is
the exquisite heart-breaking
liaison of life and love and death —
on this last dying day of the old year
bride and groom make of this inn
an everywhere
of time and space
with funeral.

We eat and drink and gossip on.
I raise a glass that is still warm,
propose a health extending
either side
of the dark river —

be with us, poet, in our earthly traffic —
Sláinte na mbeo is na marbh.

Michael Coady was born in 1939 in Carrick-on-Suir, Co Tipperary where he has lived all his life. He is the author of six collections of poetry published by The Gallery Press, most recently One Another *(2003) and* Going by Water *(2009), which integrate poetry, prose and photographs in an innovative form he has made his own. He is a member of Aosdána.*

A CANDLE IN MONTENEGRO

Paddy Bushe

i.m. *Seamus Heaney*

Near Bijelo Polje, the morning after poetry
In festive streets, a stone's throw from the square
Where flags and statues still hold their own,
We lit a candle in a dark, medieval church.

The beeswax smelt of plenitude, of time enough,
Like a judgement of ripeness. And yet the day
Outside glared, baring its teeth at the dark
Mountains that had darkened further at the news.

Later, when we read about that last text message,
Personal enough to speak to the whole wide world,
I thought of our candle guttering in the shadows
Below the peeling walls where haloed figures gleamed.

Noli timere. Now we must, as ever, trust the words,
The hand that wrote, the heart blown forever open.

Paddy Bushe was born in Dublin in 1948, and now lives in Waterville, Co Kerry. He writes in both Irish and English, and has published eight collections of poetry, most recently To Ring in Silence: New and Selected Poems *(The Dedalus Press, 2008), a bilingual volume, and* My Lord Buddha of Carraig Eanna *(The Dedalus Press, 2012).*

MERLE

Kathleen Jamie

Thon blackbird in the briar
               by the outfield dyke
doesn't know he's born,
       doesn't know he's praise and part
of this Sabbath forenoon
                north Atlantic style.
From his yellow beak his song descends
           to spring's first celandines;
his throat patters. With a yellow claw
he scarts his left lug
          without interrupting his flow …
Soon the haar will burn off
      revealing the Rum Cuillin
happed in March snow, and the waters of the Minch
      but for now the blackie's
the centre of the world's eye,
         till there! He's flown.

Celebrated as an essayist and travel writer as well as one of Scotland's foremost poets, Kathleen Jamie was born in Renfrewshire in 1952 and attended Edinburgh University. She is the author of ten collections of poetry, most recently The Overhaul *(Picador, 2012). Much of her poetry and prose pays close attention to the natural world, and her recent volume of essays,* Sightlines *(Sort of Books, 2012), won the annual Orion Book Award, a global prize. She lives in Fife.*

OPERATION

Katie Donovan

In the hospital,
gowned in gauzy cloth,
he is prepped;
his limbs so thin,
his head bursting with the tumour,
with knowing that wrestling
the thing out may kill him.

All day the cutters and stitchers
are at work, slicing from lip
to clavicle, sawing bone,
careful not to snick an artery,
gouging a flap from his thigh
to patch the gap
where the tumour hid
thriving in its secret lair.

When it's out —
and they have fixed the jaw
with a steel plate;
rivetted the long L-shape
of the wound —
he lies arrayed
with tubes and drains.
He floats in the shallows
of the anaesthetic,
his breath echoing eerily
from the hole in his throat,
his face utterly still.

The night before the operation
he read *Peter Pan*
to our children,
and in the morning
he surrendered;
waving from the trolley,
as if to clutch a last particle
of the life we figured for him,
as if to let it fall.

Katie Donovan was born in Co Wexford in 1962. She studied at Trinity College Dublin and the University of California, Berkeley. Her fourth book of poetry is Rootling: New and Selected Poems *(Bloodaxe, 2010). She teaches at the Institute of Art, Design and Technology in Dún Laoghaire, Dublin, and is currently working on a novel for children.*

THE CROSSING

Seán Lysaght

And there was one who had to master
A fear of water
To manage the crossing.

He gave a coin and was motioned in,
Allowing his ash-plant
To clatter to the floor of the boat.

Other aids were abandoned in the hold,
And he thought that he too
Might pass on without support,

Though not yet. He sat exposed on the thwart
And pressed down on the board with his palms:
The cradle of the vessel seemed so frail

For what it had to accomplish.
Then a loop of rope was lifted off the stub
And anguish gripped him at the start of the drift.

But the ferryman was there behind him
Working the oar. He jabbed the handle
In short, quick strokes

At a steep angle on its stand,
As if the deep purchase of the blade
Was shadowed in the air ahead.

As they did, the timber under pressure
Made little sounds, like wicker handles
That squeak when a creel is lifted.

And so they moved across in their own grain
Of purls and eddies, slanting upstream at first
In a way the current they faced

Let them turn in a homing curve,
And just as the boat was drawing to the riverbank
A kingfisher, of all things,

Shot past like an eye of twilight.
This settled him now to leave the craft
For ground that felt steadier than ever.

Seán Lysaght was born in 1957 and grew up in Limerick. He was educated at University College Dublin, where he studied French and English. He has published six collections of poetry and a biography of the naturalist Robert Lloyd Praeger (1865–1953), The Life of a Naturalist *(Four Courts Press, 1998). His recent collections include* The Mouth of a River *(2007), a celebration of the landscape of north Mayo, and a volume of translations from Goethe,* Venetian Epigrams *(2008), both from Gallery Press. He teaches at Galway Mayo Institute of Technology, Castlebar and lives in Westport, Co Mayo.*

WIDGEON CRIES

Damian Smyth

> *the voice box*
> *like a flute stop*

Fact is: the windpipe of the heron crane
in comparison was a garden hose
even Kevin Cunningham, the saw man,
couldn't get a tune from, blowing solos

of slow and surprising raspberries
in the Parish Hall in '74.
Aaron's Rod indeed; and such auguries
of the shotgun; such ripeness of sulphur

(like the smell of the squaddies' thick jackets
that morning, shiny elbows and gun grease,
making the dresser sing in its knick-knacks;
my father's bones in the instrument case

broken, but healing in the afterlife
germane to a wounded history of air).
Fact is: mouth to mouth, each unlikely riff
matched the ungainly bird's own repertoire

note for note. Who was to know? Pedigree
like the tongue and groove of a clarinet
dislodged, left for dead in its vertebrae,
wanting an equal love to discipline it.

Born in Downpatrick, Co Down in 1962, Damian Smyth is a poet, playwright and editor. His fifth collection of poems, Mesopotamia *(Templar) and was published in 2014. He is currently Head of Literature & Drama at the Arts Council of Northern Ireland.*

TO SEAMUS HEANEY IN HEAVEN

Ignatius McGovern

When word came I was midway
in a letter to yourself …
"What's he after now?" you ask.
I had begun like Kavanagh's swan,
"head low with many apologies",
As Hamilton once wrote to Wordsworth
Occiditque legendo!
And keeping to the last
The joke I knew you would enjoy,
The one about the Greek tailor:
Euripides? Eumenides?
But you were already beyant, like Gunnar
Sharing poems with The Greats
Miłosz, Brodsky, Lowell, Auden, Yeats.

A poet and physicist, Ignatius McGovern was born in Coleraine. He received a PhD in Physics from Queen's University Belfast and has taught at the Universities of Pennsylvania and Wisconsin. He has published three collections of poetry, The King of Suburbia *(Dedalus Press, 2005),* Safe House *(Dedalus Press, 2010), and* A Mystic Dream of 4 *(Quaternia Press, 2013) — the latter a sonnet sequence based on the life of the Irish mathematician William Rowan Hamilton. He is currently Professor in the School of Physics, and Fellow, of Trinity College Dublin.*

TWO ELEGIES

John F. Deane

ON STRAND ROAD
for Seamus Heaney

Waves have been sweeping in over the sandflats
under a chilling breeze; there is a man
windsurfing, stooping like a steeplejack
into his task; the summer girls who ran

with long gendering strides over the sand
are ghosts within a book. The poet's window
looks out across the sea towards England
and the cold north; like his bird he has grown

fabulous, comes down at times to touch
the range wall for conviction. The man on the sea
relishes each crest and hollow, and each
bow bend starts out on another journey.

AN ELEGY

Flora in the roadside ditch
are boasting the water-colour purple of a pride of bishops –
vetch, knapweed, clover and the rosebay willow herb;
and I would make a poem

the way old Bruckner caught a flight of pelicans in his
Ecce sacerdos magnus ...
for eight-part choir, key magenta, though these times the spirit
slumps, mal-tended in this limping country. Now

a blackcap, fast and furtive, comes to feast on the white berries
of the dogwood hedge; bullfinch,
secretive, subdued, flit in a shock of rose-petal black and white
across the alder thicket

and I am urged to praise, willing to have the poem
speak the improbable wonderful. Today
the poet Seamus Heaney said he was leaving us for a while,
visiting high mountain pastures,

and seeing things.
I have been walking, grieved, the Slievemore heathlands
and watching a sheep-dog,
low-crouched, eager, waiting for the sheepman's whistle;

furze blazed with a cool gold flame; the sheep
were marked with blobs of red and purple dye, cumbered
with dried-in mud; while out on the bay
the crested grebe moved, masterful, in brown Connemara tweed.

*John F. Deane was born in 1943 in Achill Island, Co Mayo. He is the author of two novels
and ten collections of poems, most recently* The Instruments of Art *(2005),* A Little Book
of Hours *(2008),* Eye of the Hare *(2010), and* Snow Falling on Chestnut Hill: New
and Selected Poems, *all from Carcanet Press. In 1979, he founded Poetry Ireland, the
national poetry organization, and* Poetry Ireland Review. *He lives in Dublin.*

THE REPLY

Francis Harvey

Outside my downstairs window,
immaculate as the blank white page
I've been facing for ages now,
snow carpets the grass.
Suddenly in the winter sunshine
a small bird appears
out of nowhere and inscribes
hieroglyphs on the snow of the lawn.
I take up my pen to write a reply.

Francis Harvey, a poet and fiction-writer, was born in Enniskillen in 1925. He is the author of five collections of poetry, most recently The Boa Island Janus *(1996),* Making Space *(2000) and* Collected Poems *(2006), all from The Dedalus Press. He lives in Donegal Town, Co Donegal.*

TWO POEMS

Michael Longley

THE SNOWDROPS

Inauspicious between headstones
On Angel Hill, wintry love-
Tokens for Murdo, Alistair,
Duncan, home from the trenches,
Back in Balmacara and Kyle,
Cameronians, Gordon Highlanders
Clambering on hands and knees
Up the steep path to this graveyard
The snowdrops whiten, green-
Hemmed frost-piercers, buttonhole
Or posy, Candlemas bells
For soldiers who come here on leave
And rest against rusty railings
Like out-of-breath pallbearers.

TELLING YELLOW
after Winifred Nicholson: a found poem

Yesterday I set out
To pick a yellow bunch
To place as a lamp
On my table in dull,
Rainy weather. I picked
Iceland poppies, marigolds,
Yellow iris; my bunch
Did not tell yellow. I
Added sunflowers, canary
Pansies, buttercups,

Dandelions; no yellower.
I added to my butter-
Like mass, two everlasting
Peas, magenta pink,
And all my yellows broke
Into luminosity.
Orange and gold
And primrose each
Singing its note.

Michael Longley was the holder of the Ireland Chair of Poetry between 2007 and 2010. The rotating three-year chair was established by the Arts Councils in Ireland, Trinity College Dublin, Queen's University Belfast, and University College Dublin to recognize the exceptional achievement of Irish poets in world literature. He is the author of 14 collections of poetry, most recently The Stairwell *(Cape, 2014). He continues to live in Belfast.*

THE HOURGLASS

Alan Gillis

Time falls like rain
in the hourglass I keep turning over,
carried from the cupboard to your gingham
covered deal table, trying to pother
the grains in your swept kitchen
on my first sleepover
at yours. You ask: "One half empties, the other
fills. Now which half is happier?"

Both ends look dead by the end.
The hourglass shows how time gathers
but only lives through the movement of the sands.
Time suffocates the sphere it enters,
voids what it leaves behind.
Through a window the shadows of alders
jig across the room as you spool your reel
then roll in tinfoil two big tuna rolls.

Up before dawn so we can have lines in
the river for sunrise, the blanket
bog's surface glistens like fish skin
breathing in the moonlight.
I have read in *The Book of Great
Facts* that bogs don't grow, they accumulate
and I can believe it in my bobble hat,
borrowed twelve-eye boots and puffed jacket.

"Keep your eyes on your feet",
you say, "this'll be the making of ye."
Then a sudden sheep
gives me the skites and I slip on the scree
of the hill as it bleats
and shrieks, niddle-noddles its straggly

backside up the hillside
like a black-shawled old woman shaking her head.

Reaching higher ground I turn to look
back on the sweep of heather and sedge
quilting the slopes and sheughs
before we pass the high ridge
and traipse downhill to bait our hooks.
Lines ready at the slosh of the river edge
you turn to me in the sough of daybreak:
"Remember, take and give, give and take."

Now time has spilled its darkness over you
I could say I'm back on those pitch
black fens once again, unable to
tell a hawthorn bush from a furzy ditch,
sludging to reach the stead of you
somewhere over the ridge
among shadows, sundews and fronds,
casting in the glent of the riverbend.

But I only stayed with you that one time
because of your drinking. Under a fleering moon
in a black-shawled night sky I dream
breathing sphagnum, moorgrass and broom
enter my body, like the taste of brine.
A cold shiver. How the rain and wide-roamed
dead, rivers and wilds, give and take,
hollow as they accumulate.

Alan Gillis is a poet and critic, born in 1973 in Belfast. He is a graduate of Trinity College Dublin and Queen's University Belfast, and was previously Lecturer in Irish Literature at the University of Ulster. The author of three books of poetry, most recently Here Comes The Night *(The Gallery Press, 2010), he is currently Lecturer in English at Edinburgh University, and Editor of* The Edinburgh Review.

SEAMUS HEANEY:
NOTES ON FAME AND FRIENDSHIP

Sven Birkerts

The mattering of literature.

Seamus Heaney, the public poet, my friend – what could I say here that could not be said as well by anyone who knew and loved the man? Already I feel the prickle of possessiveness, the territorial sideways look. Getting to know him over many years, in social but also private contexts, I naturally created a picture of our friendship. It was a weave of affinities and tacit understandings, a convergence of temperaments; it was unique. What a shock, then, to find in the accounts of others – many written after his death – evidence that all that generosity and bonhomie had not been directed just at me, or at our group of friends. Seamus had been no less engaged and engaging with a good many other people over the years.

How do you be the friend of a famous person? Or, to turn it around, if you are famous, what do you do about friendship? Of course, every situation is unique and depends on personalities; there are no rules, only exceptions. Our genuine interactions are always singular, driven by all manner of considerations. Like, here, the level and nature of the fame of the person in question. Everything is relevant. Fame is, among other things, an intoxicant, affecting all who are exposed to it.

Though the degree of his fame changed – grew – a good deal during the 30 years of our knowing each other, Seamus was in fact famous for the whole of that time. When I met him in Cambridge, it was because he had accepted a one-semester-a-year position at Harvard – that on the basis of his reputation as a poet. I therefore can't fully separate the man I knew from his public aura. Not only was he already an estimable world poet in the early 1980s but, when he moved about, at least in the places I saw him moving about in, it was always (and of course he knew this) as the object of peoples' intense awareness and interest. You always know it when *someone* comes into a room, and you always knew when Seamus arrived.

The power that fame exerts – it's too easy to see it as tied to achievement and to say it is the meaning of *that* that compels the regard. For we are stirred by the presence of fame even when we don't understand (or care) what it is founded on. When someone says, "Oh my God, look who just came in!" I feel myself come to attention, never mind that the person is an actor I've never admired or in any way cared about. I turn my head indiscreetly along with everyone else; I feel the particles in the room charge up, as if we have been graced by a presence from another order. This must mean we are worthy of that grace. Our standing has been – to take Walker Percy's word – "certified."

Of course, it's one thing to ponder this in the abstract, quite another to be in the room and to feel the actual radiation, and the expectation that it creates. There is presence – maybe "aura" is not too strong of a word. Distinction. Most of us, as seen by others – insofar as we even are seen – are just ourselves in the moment, whereas the famous ones we spot wear the trail of their histories, their rumors. They are not only recognizable in that startling way that bridges realms – the realm of their notoriety with that of the present appearance – but they also carry powerful accumulations of association. We behold the person and we get the flash impressions of what *made* the person famous ...

Some of these feelings were there when I first got to know the poet and are therefore woven into the root of our knowing each other. Nor did they ever go away completely. Though they receded privately, they just could not be ignored whenever I was with the man in a public place.

———

The first time I spoke with Seamus was at a poetry reading in Cambridge back in the early 1980s. He was not himself reading, was just in the audience – I forget who the reader was. I only remember being in my seat and feeling the sweep of my gaze suddenly catch when I saw that the poet Seamus Heaney was seated just a few rows away. *Seamus Heaney.* There are moments when life goes into italics. I knew who he was – I had read some of his work; I had heard he had a visiting position at Harvard – but none of these things squared up with that indefinable distinctive *presence* that he seemed to have. I want to say: he stood out. But did he? Did he possess a distinct actual presence that I registered, or was I just projecting upon him? Projection is a powerful business. I have more than once in my life found myself marveling at some individual's obvious distinction, only to be corrected: "no, not him, the man *over there*." Oh.

In any case, there he was, a few seats over, and for the duration of the reading I was more aware of his nearby presence than of the poet reading.

When the event was over – this I remember very clearly – there was a reception at the back of the same room. I should say that back then I professed myself a great believer in fates, coincidences, destinies – all of which designate slightly different things, but which stirred together here will represent my basic state of mind. I saw it as a stroke of something that I should be standing by the cheese and crackers at the same time as the Irish poet. And it was a purposeful movement of the stars that got us into conversation. I can't remember how it started. But there we were, holding our plastic cups, Seamus being interrupted every few moments by a fellow poet or student, me abiding patiently, as if we were having a discussion that needed returning to. I don't think we were. More likely I simply did not know how to nod and step away. And my guess, thinking back, is that Seamus recognized this awkward adhering ineptitude and did nothing that would highlight it. We stood together companionably until I finally excused myself.

I had stood with the great poet, we had talked of this and that, it had not been a complete embarrassment – end of story. But no, in fact – coincidence, fate, destiny – there's more. For after I left, as I started for home, vibrating with the thrill of that encounter, I just had to take a detour to the One Potato Two Potato, the bar and restaurant down the street from the bookstore where I then worked. I sat down and ordered a beer. And, and … and who should walk in just a few minutes later but the poet? By himself. Of course he spotted me sitting there. In my hindsight analysis he had several choices available – other than turning on his heel, that is. He could have nodded, smiled, and gone about his business, which I would have expected, which I myself might have done in his place, or he could have done what in fact Seamus did, a gesture which I now see is completely in character: make his way over and ask if I wanted company.

I linger for so long on this first meeting because it was the basis of what came to be a vital friendship in my life – and because various key themes and traits of personality (his and mine) were to be discerned there. I also need to underscore my still-unschooled zealousness, for that was an agent. It was the thing that propelled me into that original conversation at the reception and also maybe persuaded the poet that here was an intense young man handy with an opinion or quip. How I must have scrambled to be worthy! Another element, though, was Seamus's surprising availability and his kind follow-through. That he would take the seat beside me and order a pint seemed unthinkable to me then. Could I have done so in his place? Not easily. I come from a more held-in and watchful cultural background. Seamus, for his part, was from a world of pints bought and toasts offered. Be that as it may, when he came over, I saw it as a far greater confirmation than it likely was.

What did we talk about? I have no distinct memory. Whatever it was, from my side I'm sure it was all about appearing worthy, being seen as a real reader and writer – otherwise how to place a claim on the man's attention? I was, at that time, beginning to write reviews. I had written an essay on Derek Walcott, a poet I knew Seamus much admired. Surely we talked about Walcott. Also, I must have asked him questions about himself, his work. As for what he was like, his manner, I know I was struck then, and again and again over the years, by a particular gesture, which was more than a gesture – was in fact part of his manner, his grain. This was Seamus's way of appearing to confide. I have observed it now in its many subtly shaded variations. His way of leaning in slightly before saying something. A check in the voice, a hesitation, as if he were questioning whether he could in fact reveal or admit something, and then deciding that yes, he could. A gesture of glancing to one side or the other, to make sure he would not be overheard. These mannerisms were habitual to Seamus, and very convincing to me, not just on that first night, but always. They made me feel singled out, deemed worthy, admitted to the circle of those in the know about these important matters. After the saying, often, would come that hint – a momentary expression – that air of "maybe I should not have spoken so freely", but this too, when brushed aside, felt like an intimacy.

That's the word I want: intimacy. Seamus had the great ability to favor people with the sense of being intimates. He created the promise of bringing you in on things, making you privy. And though this would seem to have nothing to do with his poetry, there is a way in which it relates. For isn't it a feature of this poet's use of language that the reader is brought closer to what feels like the secret of things? Not all poets manage this; not all poets seek to. And invoking immediacy asks a very particular gift. Seamus had this art with his language and with his interactions with people as well – in closed settings, with familiars, and in larger public settings, too. He made it work by transforming the settings, making them *feel* intimate. This he might do by telling sly anecdotes, and invoking in his remarks various kindred spirits – poets and friends – and also by the working of his voice, which was (how often has this been remarked) an extraordinary instrument, warm and assuring and always used with subtle inflection, often to lightly mock the ostensible gravitas of the situation.

Seamus *was* funny. Alert to – and thus inviting – humor in others, he also tipped toward going for the laugh himself. He was a raconteur, fond of recasting the witty phrasings of friends and fellow poets, and fond, too, of elaborating the contexts that made this or that line a topper. His scene-setting, and, indeed, much of his conversation, relied on facial expression, and his repertoire encompassed everything from pious sanctimoniousness and connivance to the thousand subtle gradations of self-inflation. The timing was impeccable.

———

Seamus once – surprisingly to me – brought up the sociologist Erving Goffman. Goffman was not a name I expected to find in his range of reference, though I'm not sure quite how I created my expectation, for the man's range of interests was extensive. I remember him invoking Goffman's idea of the theatricality of self-presentation, the distinct split between off-stage and on-stage behaviors. This was, I realize, the sort of thing he would have fastened on, not least because he practiced so many variations of it himself. His situation required it. Though to me, as I've said, he was a kind of famous person from the start, it's also true that he got more and more seriously famous as the years went on. New honors, invitations … the Nobel Prize. These status promotions could not be ignored, if only because his friends were at every turn making mention, toasting and praising. The narrative of Seamus's fame was almost inevitably part of the general conversation, a pretext for funny anecdotes and extended character portraits, managed with a fine artfulness – but requiring, always, deft navigation of the shifting boundaries between those public and private realms. How did he manage this so expertly?

To begin with, primary to everything, was the Seamus air – to some degree assumed, but also I believe authentic and defining (if this is not a contradiction) – of being an innocent. A country boy, a bit rough around the edges, never not, in Wordsworth's phrase "surprised by joy." He was awarded the Nobel Prize for Literature, yes. But for all that, it somehow did not seem a downward affectation that he would tuck his napkin into his collar like a bib when he ate. That *was* Seamus, it flashed his rural Derry origins to everyone present. And by the same token, he could announce some new honor or prize – an invitation from the Empress of Japan – with such evident unmasked delight that all was forgiven from the threshold.

Given how many honors came his way, it's amazing how little he came in for deprecatory asides behind his back (at least in my experience). His joy was of such a nature that one felt compelled to share in his pleasure, not look to gainsay it.

But back to Goffman. I thought of the great sociologist and his book *The Presentation of Self in Everyday Life*, because the dynamic of 'off-stage' and 'on-stage' became more pronounced as his fame and the public demands of that fame increased. If Seamus enjoyed – and perhaps could not help – creating the chemistry of intimacy in his relations with people, so also did he take pleasure in passing back and forth over that boundary line: between public and private, scripted and natural, pretentious and humble. God knows his circumstance set him up for it. He was the Boylston Professor of Rhetoric at Harvard, but visiting him in his rooms at Adams House, you could not but notice that he had hand-washed his socks in the sink and draped them on the bathroom radiator. Yes, he loved the loosening of the tie, the putting up of the feet, the fishing around with a fork in the take-out container. He loved letting the whole charade of manners and pretences drop – by which I mean he was not just happy to stop putting on expected manners, but he liked the dropping itself, that little drop-kick administered to some bit of rigamarole at the same time as the cork was being pulled from the bottle. The fact of the former accentuated the pleasure of the latter, added to its savor.

And the pulling of that cork, the unscrewing of that cap, was a distinct pleasure, ushering in conviviality, the promise of free talk and joking. It represented stepping off the clock (for Seamus was in his working days the most organized and punctual of individuals), and waving off the constraining idea of limit. He was a great one for "one more", and it was not, I think, just that he enjoyed the drink itself – though surely he did – but also because to choose to have one more was to have no one prescribing what was enough. The gleam in his eye, the little conspiratorial smile, as he pretended to debate whether just a little splash more was not in order.

Drink – shared drink – made the stories more elaborate, the digressions more outrageous and comical, the expressions bolder, the adopted accents that much more ridiculous. The aim, for all of us, was to reach some pitch of perfect celebratory frivolity and release. What is amazing, in retrospect, is how often it was reached. Through story and joke, but also through poetry and song. The evening was not complete, it seemed, until lines – many lines – had been spoken, and some number of songs sung. Neither happened by design. It was just that one thing led to another. Poets will cite poetry – it's almost axiomatic. One cited line begetting another, the lines spoken out not as if for oral exam (though which of us did not wish for the accolade of Seamus's look of pleasure?) – but spoken because at a certain pitch of social lubrication a better language was wanted. Or else a song, an "air." And here Marie would happily oblige, as would my wife, Lynn, or the two together. Seamus would sit back and his eyes would close …

When I start writing something like this – something so dense with association – I have no idea what memories will surface. I stopped a moment ago and took a small walk to clear my thoughts, but instead of clarity there came a thronging: quick glimmers of the many things I wanted to say, or to remember so that I could linger over them, trying to find the right turns of phrase, each wondering pause the pretext for further lingering, the object of it all being the feeling that has wrapped itself around every bit of recollection. I remembered different things with every step. I wanted to focus on at Seamus's letters, the look of his handwriting – always with fountain pen, never with ballpoint … His driving, the trip he took a group of us on when a group of us went to visit him in Dublin, his solicitude. But I also flashed on certain sharp assessing moments, spikes of rancorous glee. There was a vivid image of Seamus in his cups and enraged, flinging a lit cigarette across a room at a party in Belmont. Such a weave – and with it the certainty that only some few things will get said, that all the rest, the *moiety* (and when will I ever use that word again?), will go unexpressed.

———

How did this friendship, and with it what feels like a whole distinct era, begin? What was the step between that casual first meeting over a beer and all that followed, which is to say the coming together of Seamus (and Marie) and a small group of us Cambridge-area friends – Tom Sleigh, Ellen Driscoll, Askold Melnyczuk and Alex Johnson the steady perennials – and the emergence of a durable set of relationships that continued on over many gatherings over the next 20-some years? I don't remember, quite. I know that Lynn and I hosted an early dinner party in our Cambridge apartment – that we had invited Seamus and Marie (who was visiting) as well as Derek Walcott and his wife, somehow using the fondness of the poets for each other as invitation-bait. This could not have come out of the blue. It must have followed what I remember as a series of increasingly friendly bookstore contacts. Seamus had become a regular at the Harvard Book Store where I worked the night shift. He would often arrive just at closing time, at which point a gregarious pint at One Potato Two Potato was surely in order. Certainly it would have been natural to invite a man living by himself in Harvard housing for a home-cooked meal. I'll leave it at that. An invitation was issued, Seamus accepted. When the night was over, we were on a new plateau.

The socializing continued, as socializing will, carried on across years, bridging the annual gap between June and January, the months Seamus spent back in Dublin. But what is there to say of these get-togethers? The charm and pleasure were, always, all in the occasion, the moment. What has survived, which is not negligible, is the binding memory of relaxed conversation. Laughter. Stories. The spirit of these evenings was naturally that of "off-stage", though sometimes – fairly often in fact – that atmosphere was intensified by the fact that the poet had just recently been in one of another of the situations where a more formal behavior was required. His embroidered account of the latest of these might bring us up to date and get the conversation going. Seamus liked nothing better than a set-up that let him mimic the mannerisms of a few dons or department eminences. He had a particular purse-lipped expression that captured prim rectitude perfectly. Those of us who were there when the poet and his old comrade, Seamus Deane, remembered their schooling under the priests agree we have never laughed so hard in our lives ...

But the friendship we had beyond the social evenings also interests me. What it was, but no less important, what it was *not* – what it somehow could not be. Of course I would like to rest in the conviction that we shared through those years was a rare and memorable meeting of souls, a relaxed give-and-take was that both literary and personal. And, to be sure, there were elements of that – moments of exchange that passed some pulse of understanding, sustained recognition. But there was a certain awkwardness and reticence as well. How could there not be? We had so many differences. Cultural divides, obviously. And we were 12 years apart. Seamus was too young to be the father-figure, and a bit too old to be the older brother. More of an obstacle, though, was the fame. I feel I should say it was *my* awareness of his fame, but it wasn't quite that simple. It was also Seamus's awareness of his fame and Seamus's awareness of my awareness. Mine was, and to some extent never quite stopped being, a constraint, though of course I dissimulated; I did everything I could to make it seem to count for nothing. And Seamus – how could he not at some level be responding to what he had to know was a younger man's adulation?

That is one definite price that fame does exact. It all but forces the famous person into the ongoing pretense that their status is not a major factor in his relationships with people. The charade must get exhausting on many levels – not just fine-tuning the feigned innocence of peoples' social motives, but also the pressure to appear kind and natural and thereby defeat the common assumption that of course so-and-so is going to be self-preoccupied and rude. Being famous has to be exhausting – and who will listen as you complain of the fact? It's not surprising, then, that even this fundamentally kind and genial man every so often revealed the stress of playing his role. We friends would remark it later – the distractedness, the too-ready laugh, the momentary vacancy in the expression when attention shifted away. To his enormous credit – and this, too, was a legitimate part of his achievement – he pretended kindness even when he could not have felt it. How do I know this? I don't for sure, but I noted enough darting glances to Marie at table, enough sub-audible sighs on departure. Enough that I could not imagine myself, or any of us, completely exempt.

Indeed, how could we be? We cloyed with our eagerness and flatteries, got tedious as we trotted out our arsenals of obvious reference. Everyone gets tired of everyone; no one gets off the hook. But somehow with Seamus – maybe because of the intensity of the regard – the prospect seemed especially bitter. To be the occasion of that darting glance across the table, that slightly wincing compression of the lips. Or later – and here imagination has to take over – the tongue-lashing, the unsubtle end-of-the-night coal-raking.

I never got wind of anything that overt. I don't think any of us did. Instead, there were the periodic omissions and evasions, the tendered excuses that would later be examined for their inflections and pauses. "Did he seem mad or irritated when he called?" "No, just busy. I'm sure he has a million people to see." And of course he did. Which, of course, upped his desirability, and gave a lift of triumph when a good message came through. *Thursday is fine – perfect!* How not to succumb to a certain narcissistic preening – being out in public with Seamus, with Marie, experiencing the near-physical sensation of being checked out by curious strangers?

———

This brings reminders of Milton's invoking of fame as "last infirmity of noble minds" – a phrase that was often played off one way and another during these long evenings. It *is* an irresistible topic. For the striking thing about fame is the potent contradiction that invests it: that it is universally sought after and prized – more, I would say, even than wealth – but that the seeking, the appearance of seeking, is often a matter of shame. Hence "infirmity." There is shame because the seeking is closely bound up with covetousness, egotism, competitiveness, envy. One does not want to be seen pursuing fame, but one wants very much to have it – along with greatness – thrust upon him- or herself. And of course there is shame, too, felt by (and attaching to) those who seek to be in fame's reflected light. To be associated with the chosen person is to acquire a lunar radiance oneself. One is supposed – and maybe supposes oneself – to be worthy of the proximity. All kinds of egotism and rancor attend this relationship. Not least is the question of the underlying motivations of the attachment. "Am I drawn to X because he is famous? Would I be so solicitous if he were not?" And, from X: "Is it me they seek, or that which I have, which has been granted to me (which I have earned)?"

Complicated, yes, the whole business. There is an enormous difference between what more rightly should be called "celebrity" – though people confuse it with fame – and that status that has either been earned through accomplishment or is granted in recognition of some indisputable gift or genius. The "fame" of an ultimately incidental media figure, say, versus that of a great poet. For a person to seek out the former – or to seek to be in his or her light – is one thing, and the desires having to do with the latter are quite another.

Seamus's fame had everything to do with his obvious and exceptional literary talent, his ability to make poems that embodied their occasions with resonant accuracy, that were emotionally expressive and singular, not to be mistaken for anyone else's. Such a talent, whether refined through long craft or simply present as a kind of "gift" is felt to be a power unto itself. It is, like beauty, inexplicably magnetic. To be in the presence of beauty is, I believe, to feel pulled *toward* it, as if it is a kind of primal source. The same is true for power that we identify with artists and creators. We want to be near it. Why? Do we imagine that some of it will flake off and attach to us? Or that any recognition on the part of the possessor is also a recognition of something kindred in ourselves?

There is some truth in all of it, I'm guessing. But I would like to propose now that our responding to such a recognition is not all vanity and opportunism, either – that it represents the activation of some of our finer impulses, and is also idealistic. When I first saw Seamus at that poetry reading in Cambridge, I saw him as justly celebrated author of a number of poems that had stirred me. My excitement was also, it's true, a kind of confusion. Confusion – and this is maybe a bit exaggerated – between my experience of the poems, which are felt to be somehow outside ordinary time, and the slightly rumpled physical immediacy of their maker. But I remind myself – and believe, if only to preserve my self-esteem – that, confusion or no, the primary attraction was finally less the fact of his public notoriety and more that he was the man who had written these many great poems. As soon as the meeting happened, the acquaintance – and the eventual friendship, of course – the distinction grew blurred. But on the far side of the complex assessment of motives, intents and incentives, I believe things were clear enough. After all, here was the basis of the mattering of literature.

One of America's leading prose writers, Sven Birkerts is the author of seven books of non-fiction, including The Gutenberg Elegies: The Fate of Reading in the Electronic Age *(Faber, 1994),* Readings *(Graywolf, 1999),* My Sky Blue Trades: Growing Up Counter in a Contrary Time *(Viking, 2002) and* The Other Walk *(Graywolf, 2011). He is Editor of* AGNI *and taught at Harvard University.*

THE SILENCE OF SEAMUS HEANEY'S FATHER

Gerard McCarthy

On the tarbert.

Seamus Heaney died in 2013 as summer was giving way to autumn. His funeral mass in Dublin was broadcast live on television. It was apt, measured and moving. His fellow poet Paul Muldoon gave a eulogy, in which he used a motif of the letter B. He brought it to a close by speaking of Heaney's bardic beauty and, finally, the beauty of his being. Although no judgement is clear and simple on any human life, the image portrayed at his funeral mass of the being of the man, Seamus Heaney, was admirable and appealing; it was one of someone at harmony with himself and with those around him. God rest him.

The programme finished with the end of the mass as the mourners left the church, and the cortège was preparing for the final journey to his home place, Bellaghy. As the cortège was heading north, I was driving out west, to Mayo, to cross to one of the small islands in inner Clew Bay. My departure had been precipitate, and the journey had an element of flight about it. It was only as I passed through Westport, when the sunshine that had prevailed for most of the day gave way to drizzle, that I realised that I had left my normal glasses behind me and had brought only the prescription sunglasses I was wearing. As I drove down to where my currach was moored, Heaney's play, *The Burial at Thebes*, was coming onto the car radio. I parked and walked in the drizzle to the mooring where the currach was waiting. It was misting heavily on the short journey across. I could barely make out the island mooring. I landed, pulled the boat out and headed up to the old schoolhouse. I lit a fire, and listened timorously to the rest of *The Burial at Thebes*. I stood outside for a little while when it was over but, between the drizzle and the dark glasses, I could see only obscurely the regular flashing of the lighthouse on Inishgort, and inside it the erratic flashing of the light at the jetty that used to light the way for Sean Jeffers, that now lights the way for no one. In the schoolhouse I lit candles and focussed my attention inside for the rest of the evening. Before bed, I read Heaney's late poem, "Uncoupled", which I had downloaded onto my laptop.

It has two deeply fond vignettes from the depths of his childhood: of his mother in the first verse, and of his father in the second. The poem ends with the memory of his father, in a loud confusion of cattle, turning his attention away from his eldest son to the adult world around him: the first speechless loss of the poet, that the poem six decades later redeems.

I woke a number of times during the longish night with the uneasiness of an animal alone in the dark. I dreamed the house of my own childhood was still standing and that years after his death my father had returned and was living his life as an old man. We were all celebrating the miracle of it. I caught his glance just before I was leaving and basked in his warm approval. Then, as I went out the door, I cast another glance back for a further glance from him, but his attention was deflected by the crowd around him. I woke, holding on to the memory of the image of the previous glance. Although I couldn't remember the occurrence, it seemed that the dream was the echo of a memory.

The figure of the father is fundamental to the poetic dimension that Seamus Heaney retained of his religion. He alludes to this in the series of interviews he gave to Dennis O'Driscoll, in the closing chapter of the book, called *Stepping Stones*. He was responding to two quotes from Wallace Stevens about the close kinship between religion and poetry. Stevens had said that God is a symbol for something that could as well take the form of high poetry. Included in Heaney's response were the following three statements: "poetry is the ratification of the impulse towards transcendence"; "poetry represents the need for an ultimate court of appeal"; and, *pace* Pascal's dread of the eternal silence of the infinite spaces, "there has to be something more than neuter absence." Having lost the transcendent faith he had inherited from his father, he saw the making of poetry as the ratification of the impulse. His mention of an ultimate court is a reference to his poem, "The Stone Verdict"; he goes on to quote it: how his father would expect more than words in the ultimate court he relied on through a lifetime's speechlessness. He said that he imagined the celestial silence beyond us as a divine corrective to human protestation: the silence behind the silence of his father, which his own lifetime's profession had breached.

The morning after Seamus Heaney's funeral I went walking on the island. The sky was lightening. There were pools of pale September sunlight scattered around the bay. From the hill of the near headland I noticed two in particular, one around the lighthouse on Clare Island, and the other around the near lighthouse on Inishgort. In front of the lighthouse I could see clearly the house of Sean Jeffers, the last of the line of men who in their time had tended it. To the south, above the bay, Croagh Patrick was shrouded. Nearby, on the tarbert, I saw Brendan Joyce cutting wrack: a familiar figure in the bay for decades, he had disappeared for some years during the mad dream of the first decade of the millennium, working on the mainland during the economic bubble, driving a lorry for a builder. Now he had returned, and his distant figure, bent down, silently cutting the wrack from the rocks, was once again a deeply characteristic image of the life of the bay. Later, as I stood in the schoolhouse doorway, I saw him passing in his boat, pulling his bale of wrack, waiting for the tide to rise before he brought the harvest of his day's labour into the shore at Rosmindle. Our salute was the prolonged and emphatic one between boat and shore of good will at a distance.

Autumn of 2013 gave way to winter. It was a mild one, most memorable for the storms, and for the sea surge in January 2014 which caused devastation along the west coast of Ireland. Cars were washed off the pier at Cleggan, and a bridge near Rosmoney was swept away by the flood tide receding. A month later, at the following big strand, a few of us walked across the tarbert to the island. The big tide had divided the island in two, and had left seaweed for the first time inside the gate of the schoolhouse. We had an hour there on either side of the low tide turning. On our way back, I saw Brendan Joyce off at a distance, cutting wrack. I had a hailed exchange with him. We bemoaned the storms. He shouted that the sea had risen five foot above the road down to our common mooring, and he said the likelihood was that there is worse to come. I shouted back that it was as well in that event that we have boats. The wind got up then and I couldn't hear his reply, if there was one, and immediately I regretted my facetiousness about something of much more immediate material concern to him than to me.

A while later I joined a gathering of old cronies in a pub. All of us shared in common that we had been born in Dublin in the middle of the last century, and had spent the bulk of our adult lives in the west of Ireland. There was talk of the winter floods, and of the question of global warming. We agreed we are unlikely to see a global catastrophe in our lifetimes. We remembered our shared past: how our lives had been greatly privileged in their stability and economic security, despite the turbulence of the wider world. We acknowledged the transient bubble blown up by the suburban

Dublin of our adolescent world as the 1960s gave way to the 70s, with the sudden impact of the wider world. There was mention of the death of Seamus Heaney. In one of his interviews he had spoken of being fully formed by 1963; there had been for some of us a childish tendency to see him as belonging to a previous generation. Although in awe of the fecundity of his wordsmithery, he had seemed to be part of the Irish Catholic world we were turning our backs on. We remembered our assault on the axioms of our inheritance, and how we wholeheartedly applauded when the man sang to the mothers and fathers throughout the land, not to criticise what they couldn't understand. We remembered how we saw ourselves as on the cusp of a new world, until our worlds became amorphous.

Winter gave way to spring. A good spell of weather dried out the land, and in the nature of things the real presence of the winter floods sank back in people's memory. Out of the blue I found myself back on the island on a balmy May evening. I sat outside the schoolhouse watching two herons on the mouldering gables of the ruined cottage close by; they looked to my eyes like oriental monkeys. I walked over the shore to gain a closer look, but they languorously lifted themselves and flew off at my approach. As I stood by the gable I remembered Seamus Heaney's poem, "The Stone Verdict": after the first verse, with its Christian image of the final court, the second turns to a metaphor from the ancient Greek world and imagines the father's apotheosis in the silence of such a ruined homestead. The silence of stone. My evening in the schoolhouse was wordless. I paid a brief visit over to the beach at twilight. The water was still, and there was silence but for the rhythm of a slight wash on some distant shore. The lighthouse had begun flashing, and the light above Sean Jeffers's jetty was still going on and off without rhyme or reason. I went outside in the middle of the night and saw the dark vault studded with crystal. In the middle of it all, directly above the schoolhouse, there was the amorphous glistening of the centre of the galaxy that one small island of life has named the Milky Way.

At dawn the cloud cleared into a beautiful May morning. There was a cool breeze but the sun was shining. Swallows and starlings were flitting around the house, and on the hill the larks: the larks were rising. I saw Brendan Joyce coming out of the mouth of Rosmindle. His figure and his boat were a glimmering shadow in a huge flood of sunlight. I marvelled his dedication and commitment: his long day of hard silent physical work on a Sunday as I sauntered the near headland. The view was expansive, deeply familiarly. One lark rose straight in front of me at the top of the hill, singing its heart out as it climbed almost perpendicularly, until it drifted a little before it glided downward again, landing where I could see it again right in front of me. Halfway down the far side of the hill, as I was walking past a thicket of brambles and gorse, I heard a bark, and when I looked I saw the light brown reddish hind-quarters of a fox disappear into the undergrowth, its bark presumably a warning to its own kind on seeing an intruder.

The bark of the island fox: it seemed a summons to a *laudate*; a sound beyond the human world, taking me beyond the thicket of thought. I sat on a bank looking out. There was thin cloud overhead, but Clare Island was bathed in sunlight. Above the bay the Reek was dark but the church on top of it was gleaming. For moments I gained glimpses of the purity of the manifestation of the world of the islands around me. I remembered Seamus Heaney's comment about how there has to be more than neuter absence in the vastness; I thought how the flamboyant light and life and colour that I saw around me was as close to the centre of the universe as anywhere else — as intimate, as intrinsic.

As I was heading down to the currach, Brendan was coming along slowly in his boat, pulling another bale of wrack behind him in the rising tide. He was taking it slow, minding his load. He asked me had there been a lot of water in the currach as there had been a woeful amount of rain last night. I asked him had he cut all of the bale of wrack that day and when he said he had I complimented him on the hard work he had done on a Sunday. He asked, "Do you think, the Man Above, do you think He'll let me in?" I said I thought He would. He laughed. "Do you think He'll take pity on me?" I assured him I was sure He would, and our leavetaking was a shared laughter as I pulled on past him, in through the mouth of Rosmindle, back out to the wider world.

Gerard McCarthy works as a social worker in the West of Ireland. His first published essays, "Old Istanbul", "Old Jerusalem", "Home from Andalucia" and "The Road to Granada", appeared in earlier issues of Irish Pages.

ETHICAL DEPTH

Manus Charleton

Moral excellence.

In its award of the Nobel Prize for literature in 1995 to Seamus Heaney, the Swedish Academy praised his poetry's "lyrical beauty and ethical depth, which exalt everyday miracles and the living past." It's easy to appreciate why the academy cited the poetry's lyrical beauty; less easy perhaps to see why they cited ethical depth. There is an ethical note, one which readers (and listeners) pick up, and to cite ethical depth as a prominent characteristic feels right. At the same time, it's a curious choice, for ethics isn't usually associated with poetry. Nor is it obvious what ethical depth means or how it features in the poems.

There are aspects to his personal history which would have honed ethical sensibility and tuned the ethical note. They include gratitude to his parents; appreciation of the opportunity to receive a university education as the first in his family; obligation to others who hadn't been as fortunate; neighbourliness; and, from the death of his four-year-old brother, an awareness while still a schoolboy of how frail and precious life is. Also, there are values associated with traditional rural living in Ireland, such as decency, kindness and generosity of spirit which by all accounts were marks of the man, and they are qualities which can be detected in the tenor of the poems.

This is not to see the poetry as old-fashioned and out of tune with his time when the pace of technological change was accelerating and there was a turn away from valuing community bonds towards individualism. For these values, though ever fragile, are natural and necessary threads in the social fabric. As Edmund Burke saw them in his eloquent description, the values make for "all the decent drapery of life," drapery which "the heart owns and the understanding ratifies, as necessary to cover the defects of our naked shivering nature, and to raise it to dignity, in our own estimation." Burke feared the drapery would be swept away by French revolutionary violence. He also called the drapery "superadded ideas, furnished from the wardrobe of moral imagination." And, after centuries of moral essentialism arising from religion and from some moral philosophies, to understand a source for the ideas of values in the capacity of moral imagination is to draw them close to the arts and give them a contemporary feel and appeal.

Growing up in Ulster, Seamus Heaney also experienced justice out of joint. And, during the decades of political and sectarian conflict, there was helplessness in the face of spiralling violence in which the common language of ethical reasoning and pleading, along with the language of conciliatory politics, was constantly pushed to its limits in trying, and failing, to be effective. In some of the poems we hear him wrestling with his conscience about how he should respond, in particular as the violence affects the community from which he has come and one of his cousins is killed. But it's his sense of what poetry specifically can and should do ethically that wins out. It's not hard to imagine an in-driven need to create a deep-seated poetic place which would reflect a strong sense of ethics beyond the rupturing political realities, one which boosts the already-present aesthetic need for unity in a work. And in his essay "Feeling into Words" he refers to the "imperative" he felt after the violence of the summer of 1969 "to discover a field of force in which, without abandoning fidelity to the processes and experience of poetry … it would be possible to encompass the perspectives of a humane reason and at the same time to grant the religious intensity of the violence its deplorable authenticity and complexity."

"Humane reason" did become characteristic of the work. It gives to the lyrical note its sturdiness. And, from his rural, farming background, he experienced the value of honest toil, with its hardships and satisfactions. It is inherent in a number of poems, early on in "The Forge" and in "Digging", and carried over into how he saw the work of the artist. It is part of the ethical note which comes through a certain even-handed treatment of content in a unifying sound of carefully weighted syllables.

Towards the end of his working life, asked by Dennis O'Driscoll in *Stepping Stones* what poetry had taught him, he said that "poetry itself has virtue." It has it "in the sense of possessing a quality of moral excellence." From the Greek *arete*, "virtue" means "excellence" or "power", and it is in this sense we can begin to see it as a quality of poetry. A poem has excellence in being well made, in being fitting or adequate to its purpose, like a good piece of household furniture. Crafted excellence is a quality carried in the plain speaking in the opening lines of the first stanza of "The Bookcase":

Ashwood or oakwood? Planed to silkiness.
Mitred, much-eyed along, each vellum-pale
Board in the bookcase held and never sagged.

In "vellum" we can hear time-honoured tradition, and in the final line of the stanza is the direct statement: "Virtue went forth from its very shipshapeness."

In the biblical "went forth" there is an intimation of something holy or sacred, and he has referred to what he called his "Catholic imagination." Catholicism was the faith in which he was raised, and its practices and imagery are in his poetry. But his imagination is not Catholic in any restrictive, denominational sense. While religious or spiritual in association, the poems which touch us with a sense of being in the presence of the mysterious or miraculous do so in a way which is open-ended and universal. In his response to the question of what poetry had taught him, he saw a poem having virtue "in the sense also of possessing inherent strength by reason of its sheer made-upness, its *integritas*, *consonatia* and *claritas*." These are the qualities of wholeness, harmony and radiance, the qualities Aquinas identified in his *Summa Theologica* as necessary for beauty in a work of art. In referring to them Seamus Heaney is not aligning his poetic aesthetic to Catholic theology, but echoing Stephen Dedalus in *A Portrait of the Artist as a Young Man*, where Stephen sees the qualities corresponding to "the necessary phases of artistic apprehension."

As for the "power" which the Greeks associated with virtue, it exists not just with the force that deploying the right word in the right place can have, with the *mot juste*, but also with the magical and oracular, with the effect an inspired combination of words and sounds in a poem can give off. Among his achievements is to have revived in a modern period of downbeat realism, and in a postmodern one of mixum-gatherum experimentation, poetry's power as high art, while simultaneously finding and giving voice to the glimmerings of this power in the ordinary and the everyday – in a spade, a school satchel, a kite. His essay "Mossbawn" begins with an account of the significance of *omphalos* which the hand-pump had in the backyard of his family's farmhouse. A hand-pump as much an auditory centre as a visual one, for, when it's pumped, *omphalos* comes onomatopoetically from "its blunt and fallen music." In this sense of power too, poetry has virtue, the power to lift restriction and transport us imaginatively.

There is a human propensity to have a relation to something of ultimate value which transcends us. Asked by O'Driscoll whether he would agree with Wallace Stevens about the idea of God as a symbol which can take other forms, such as the form of high poetry, Seamus Heaney said he had no doubt about that. Then he said: "Poetry is the ratification of the impulse towards transcendence." The directed, magnetic pull of attention inherent in the propensity towards transcendence is perhaps at its most intimate in the lines from "Station Island" where, in a church, we're given a sense of being halted on the threshold of the ineffable:

> There was an active, wind-stilled hush, as if
> in a shell the listened-for ocean stopped
> and a tide rested and sustained the roof.

In "Station Island" he also gives us an image of being gripped and moved by a sense of some ultimate source beyond words that, although associated with absence, has the uplifting effect of transcendent experience:

> A cold draught blew under the kneeling boards.
> I thought of walking round
> and round a space utterly empty,
> utterly a source, like the idea of sound;
>
> like an absence stationed in the swamp-fed air
> above a ring of walked-down grass and rushes
> where we once found the bad carcass and scrags of hair
> of our dog that had disappeared weeks before.

In "Clearances 8" he develops the sense of being gripped by transcendent experience. A chestnut tree he has grown from seed is cut down, which brings on a repeat of the lines about the thought of walking round and round a space utterly empty and utterly a source. But now the "heft and hush" the tree once had have become "a bright nowhere, / A soul ramifying and forever / Silent, beyond silence listened for."

The way to the experience of something transcendent isn't the exclusive preserve of theistic religious faiths through their rituals, liturgy and morality. Nor does it require spiritual transportation onto some ethereal plane that negates or devalues our inherence in this world. As he shows, the impulse towards transcendence is earthy and primordial and can culminate in an intimation of some ultimate source reached through our experience of the physicality of things. The impulse is born and persists in the very movement of exploring the physical world though our senses. This is detectable in "Bogland". The opening lines summon visual depth to our imagination by contrasting Ireland's variegated topography, in which the eye gives way to, and is held in by, successive features, with flatlands in other countries which afford an expansive gaze:

> We have no prairies
> To slice a big sun at evening –
> Everywhere the eye concedes to
> Encroaching horizon,
>
> Is wooed into the Cyclops eye
> Of a tarn.

After the striking visual image in the first two lines, the following ones blend a reflective observation about what happens in visual perception with a feeling of sight moving across a landscape and alighting on an object. "Wooed" has imaginative sweep, with its intimations of seduction, inescapable desire and apprehension. And "Cyclops" hits us with arresting force as the perfect word for a tarn, for he is the one-eyed mythological giant of brute strength and power who, in holding us in his sight, can make us quake, and yet he concentrates for us awareness of the power of vision and of focus, of the gaze on the world; the power too of the gaze of God as he exists in story and in ontology and theology, if not in reality. As the poem proceeds it opens out and opens down with a sense of giving way. The bog is "unfenced" and is melting "black butter" underfoot. It's a store-ground of the past where discovered remains bring us up in fresh astonishment in the face of nature, as exemplified by the sight of the Great Irish elk whose skeleton is set up "An astounding crate full of air." And beneath the layering, the ultimate source is pointed towards beyond words, for "The wet centre is bottomless."

———

His writings also show him addressing the question of the ethical import of poetry in a world in which there is much inhumanity, a question which concerned him in particular in the essay "The Redress of Poetry", and also in "The Poetic Redress", his introduction to the book of writings by different authors on the UN Declaration of Human Rights. And we can see how his reflections would have contributed to shaping the poetry. He writes about the significance for him of the idea he found in Simone Weil's book *Gravity and Grace* of trying to add to the lighter pan on the scales which is outweighed by the heavier pan of injustice and distress. As redress, poetry can be "a counterweight to the given actuality of the world" in which violations of rights take place. Yet poetry is its own *métier*, and has to be if it is to succeed. It withers as a mouthpiece for moral criticism or sentiment, and dies in didactics. Instead, poetry works ethically by carrying within it a correspondence with the movement we recognise as ethical in which there is realisation of potential in a way that is both freeing and directed:

> In this "redress" there is no hint of ethical obligation; it is more a matter of finding a course for the breakaway of innate capacity, a course where something unhindered, yet directed, can sweep ahead into its full potential.

And it's because poetic form is its own *métier* that, as he said in his Nobel speech, it has "the power to persuade the vulnerable part of our consciousness of its rightness in spite of the evidence of wrongness all around it ..."

The power and responsibility of conscience is the theme of the poem "From the Republic of Conscience". In the opening stanza, after the plane lands and its engines stop and it is "so noiseless," there's an image of the arresting call of conscience when the poet hears "a curlew high above the runway." A metaphysical atmosphere is conveyed from the description of the country's strangeness and the way they do things there, such as when the poet is shown a photograph of his grandfather by the clerk at the immigration desk who is an old man. And in the last stanza, as the poet is leaving, the clerk having desired him to consider himself a representative of the Republic of Conscience, he is told "its embassies were everywhere" and "operated independently and no ambassador would ever be relieved."

The idea of conscience as something akin to a compelling call or a voice is deeply embedded in culture and still with us as a good working metaphor. Its roots are in the Classical literature of the fifth century bc, in Plato's account of Socrates' *daimon*, the intermediary guiding spirit Socrates felt between him and the gods who indicates the path of virtue, and who gave him the inner strength to undergo martyrdom in the cause of freedom to pursue the truth through open dialogue. Seamus Heaney's writings draw from the richness of the Classical world, nowhere more so than in *The Cure of Troy: After Philoctetes by Sophocles*. In his version he gives contemporary relevance to the theme of how deep-rooted ethical/psychological difficulty blocks the ending of conflict. The difficulty is all the more stubborn to overcome when the wound suffered is bound up with a whole people. The vent through which personal conscience breathes becomes constricted. It's not merely that, in justice, we find it hard to let go the tight grip of festering hurt from a wound others have inflicted on us, but that in some way resentment towards the enemy also seems to vindicate us to ourselves. For such recalcitrant wounds, the cure lies in realising hope "for a great sea-change" in which desire for vengeance is overcome so that "a farther shore / Is reachable from here."

The human rights described in international covenants are underpinned by deep roots. Seamus Heaney sees rights as having their origin in the metaphysical. Referring to the UN Declaration, he asks in "The Poetic Redress":

> How else, indeed, could the document enshrine words like "dignity" and "conscience", words which strain against the bonds of legal definition and political categorisation?

While we can sense that rights have an indefinable metaphysical origin, they are also directly connected to our needs for survival and well-being. Our basic needs and humanity suffer when rights are overridden, such as happened when the ideals of state socialism were forcibly imposed. The metaphysical origin underlies and gives strength to the necessity and appeal we associate with ethics, whether by way of human rights or other expressions of value, and to which the ideas of the moral imagination are beholden. In "The Redress of Poetry" Seamus Heaney refers to Plato's questioning of the usefulness and justification of poetry in the *polis*, a *polis* which Plato conceived as a tightly ordered ideal republic. Nonetheless, he refers to the metaphysical world of Plato's ideal forms, which include those of beauty and goodness, as providing "the court of appeal through which poetic imagination seeks to redress whatever is wrong or exacerbating in the prevailing conditions."

It is because poetry can convey a sense of ethical roots, including ratification of the impulse towards something of ultimate value in transcendence that, in a phrase he has used, it "fortifies inwardness." It gives us a hold on the endurance of the roots and of the impulse. We can turn to it for support when particular acts and events take us apart. "Anything can happen" are the opening words of the poem "Horace and the Thunder (after Horace, Odes 1, 34)". And in the essay, "Reality and Justice: On Translating Horace" (republished in the "Justice" issue of *Irish Pages* under the heading "Keeping Us Right", along with the poem), he writes of the power of art to hold its ground in the face of terrible events. When put to the test, it is able "to keep itself whole and its viewers hale" through "its capacity to distinguish itself from us and our needs and at the same time to make our needs and ourselves distinct and contemplatable."

We can envisage him concurring with Iris Murdoch's Platonic observation in *Metaphysics as a Guide to Morals*:

> The art-object, transcendent, clarified, self-contained, alone, secure and time-resistant, shedding light upon the miserable human scene, prompting compassion and just judgment, seems like a picture of goodness itself, a sort of semi-sensory image of a spiritual ideal.

Manus Charleton lectures in Ethics and Politics at the Institute of Technology, Sligo. He is the author of the textbook Ethics for Social Care in Ireland: Philosophy and Practice *(Gill and Macmillan, 2007). He has been published previously in* Irish Pages, *in the* Dublin Review of Books *and in* Studies: An Irish Quarterly Review.

"STATION ISLAND": A KIND OF VALEDICTION

Patricia Craig

All standing waiting.

Thinking about Seamus Heaney recently, I found some lines from Section Five of "Little Gidding" coming into my head. Eliot is setting out a prescription for a kind of perfection, not easily attainable, a rare felicity of tone and content. It occurs, he says, when:

> … every word is at home,
> Taking its place to support the others,
> The word neither diffident nor ostentatious,
> An easy commerce of the old and the new,
> The common word exact without vulgarity,
> The formal word precise but not pedantic,
> The complete consort dancing together.

"The complete consort dancing together." I think that almost everything Heaney wrote, in a long writing career, entirely conforms to Eliot's specification. I'm including his prose here no less than his poetry, but just for the moment I'd like to concentrate on a particular poem – "Station Island" – which, as we know, owes something to "Little Gidding", as well as to Dante's *Divine Comedy*: although, as Heaney said himself, there's no heaven or hell about it, only purgatory. St Patrick's Purgatory, to be precise, at Lough Derg in County Donegal, a place of pilgrimage from the twelfth century on and associated, in my mind at least, with devout middle-aged women in headscarves on their knees intoning rosaries, scrawny men wearing Pioneer Total Abstinence badges in their lapels, and browbeaten schoolchildren. Not that I ever set foot in the place or felt the smallest inclination to do so. As a Dominican pupil on the Falls Road in Belfast in the 1950s, I was well schooled in the ways of Catholic affirmation; but I and most of my contemporaries drew the line at Lough Derg. We weren't penitentially inclined. In so far as I'd be entitled to lay claim to any part of Donegal, it would not be bleak, ominous Lough Derg with the basilica and assorted buildings looming on the island in the middle of the lake like some medieval penitentiary – not that, but the Irish-speaking areas of Rannafast, Loughanure and Teelin, which, as far as I was concerned, had a countervailing spirit of pungency and exhilaration about them. In his "Stations of the West", Heaney falls under the spell of a few of these place-names too: "Rannafast and Errigal, Annaghry and Kinkasslagh" – names, he goes on "portable as altar stones." And, in the same small collection of what you might call prose poems, *Stations*, published in 1975, which Heaney describes as "points on a psychic *turas*", or journey, there's one – a rather cryptic one – entitled "Patrick and Oisin". In the Irish poetry book we used at school, *Filíocht na nGael*, there was one poem which struck a chord with me. Well, there were many, but I remember this one in particular, "Lon Doire an Chairn", "The Blackbird of Derrycairn", partly because it wasn't on the school curriculum. Its final quatrain has unrepentant Oisín upholding a remembered Fenian exultation in the face of a creeping Christian pusillanimity exemplified in the dire sound of the church bell: one in the eye for St Patrick and his wretched Purgatory (before it existed).

> An trath do mhair Fionn 's an Fhiann'
> Dob ansa leo sliabh na chill,
> Ba bhinn leosan fuighle lon,
> Gutha na gclog leo niorbh' bhinn.

So – no Lough Derg pilgrimage for us free spirits, as we considered ourselves, thank you very much. Seamus Heaney, on the other hand, had personal experience of the Station Island carry-on; although, as he indicates, when he went there as a Queen's student among a crowd of Catholic fellow-students, the breast-beating aspect of the place of pilgrimage was tempered by an irrepressible sense of excursion and element of flirtation: it wasn't wholly holy. As the shade of Patrick Kavanagh puts it in Heaney's version: "In my own day / The odd one came here on the hunt for women."

Well! If they did, you might think, they were being unduly optimistic; Lough Derg with its requirements of fasting and praying, its sleep-deprived nights and barefoot treks around the stony Station "Beds", would never have afforded much of an outlet for amorousness. However, as an emblem, St Patrick's Purgatory lends itself to more than one interpretation. I was delighted, for example, when I first read William Carleton's story, "The

Lough Derg Pilgrim", which confirms the existence of Catholic chicanery as far back as the early 1800s, and leaves the protagonist, a stand-in for Carleton himself, utterly disillusioned with the whole religious gallimaufry. "There is no specimen of Irish superstition equal to that which is to be seen at St Patrick's Purgatory in Lough Derg", goes the stern verdict of the narrator. Outraged of the Clogher Valley. Carleton's inspiriting story got absorbed into the lore of Lough Derg and must have been in the mind of every subsequent half-literate pilgrim to the place; as Heaney puts it in Section Two of his poem, addressing the shade of Carleton, "Your *Lough Derg Pilgrim* / Haunts me every time I cross this mountain – / as if I am being followed, or following. / I'm on my road there now to do the station" – drawing, as I've said before, a robust retort from the doughty old turncoat: "Oh holy Jesus Christ, does nothing change!"

Richard Ellman, writing in the *New York Review of Books*, judged "Station Island" to be Heaney's most ambitious work to date, with its author's "prodigious talent" now "exfoliating and augmenting." We can go along with this, but I don't think he was quite right to call the poem "an act of self-accusation." It's more in the line, as Heaney himself observed, of an examination of conscience – the procedure that comes before the act of confession in the Catholic catechism. And here the religious dimension of the thing is recast in secular terms, with historical, literary, political, autobiographical, even topographical undercurrents making for an invigorating and illuminating approach. In so far as "self-accusation" comes into it, I'm reminded (again) of the words attributed to Eliot's "familiar compound ghost" in "Little Gidding", when he talks about

> the rending pain of reenactment
> Of all that you have done, and been; the shame
> Of motives late revealed, and the awareness
> Of things ill-done and done to others' harm
> Which once you took for exercise of virtue.

These lines, of course, are especially applicable to Section Eight of "Station Island" and the voice attributed to Heaney's murdered second cousin Colum McCartney, who rounds on the poet with the lacerating indictment,

> The Protestant who shot me through the head
> I accuse directly; but indirectly, you

who now atone perhaps upon this bed
for the way you whitewashed ugliness and drew
the lovely blinds of the *Purgatorio*
and saccharined my death with morning dew

This refers back to Heaney's elegy "The Strand at Lough Beg" in the 1978 collection *Field Work* – which falls short, perhaps, in the areas of outrage and outright condemnation of the sectarian atrocity; though I think the Heaney of "Station Island" is being a bit too hard on Heaney the lyricist, whose impulse is not so much to sweeten as to dignify. And, as Heaney's friend Karl Miller said, "there are many ways for a poet to be political", and some of these ways are more oblique than others.

The significant shades of "Station Island", including Colum McCartney, an old Anahorish schoolmaster, an archaeologist friend and an old girlfriend, add up to a kind of compound image of the poet's inheritances (political and otherwise), his affiliations, affirmations and repudiations. The sum total of Heaney's familiar ghosts creates an effect unlike that of Eliot's "familiar compound ghost", in so far as the latter boils down in large measure to the single figure of W.B. Yeats. (I'll get to Yeats's absence from, and Joyce's presence in, "Station Island" in a moment.) Heaney's personal ghosts – some of which I've just mentioned – are crucial to the poem's drift and pulse; but what is equally central to it is the presence of literary antecedents, starting – as I've said – with William Carleton.

Which brings me to the theme of continuity. When the narrator of "Station Island" reports to William Carleton's ghost,

... A lot of what you wrote
I heard and did: this Lough Derg station,
flax-pullings, dances, summer crossroads chat

And the shaky local voice of education.
All that. And always, Orange drums.
And neighbours on the roads at night with guns

Heaney is attesting to the persistence of country lore and traditions, at least up until the period of his own childhood in the 1940s and 1950s. We have continuity and tradition on the one hand, and on the other, inescapably, contemporary attitudes and complexities, all of which are bound up with the energy and resonance of "Station Island". And, while Heaney's early experience may resemble Carleton's in certain respects – "Oh holy Jesus Christ, does nothing change!" – what each makes of it is down to the individual consciousness, the singular *modus operandi*.

Some verses after Carleton in the "Station Island" sequence comes Patrick Kavanagh, another one-time Lough Derg pilgrim who addresses the poet in a manner half ironic and half belligerent:

> Sure I might have known
> once I had made the pad, you'd be after me
> sooner or later. Forty-two years on
> and you've got no farther!

Dr Peter Kavanagh, in his 1978 introduction to the long poem *Lough Derg*, insists his brother went to Station Island in search of "spiritual renewal" – but if he did, Patrick Kavanagh couldn't resist taking note, at the same time, of the mundane aspirations driving the bulk of his fellow pilgrims:

> A woman said in her litany: ...
> That my daughter Eileen may do well at her music
> We beseech Thee to hear us
> That her aunt may remember us in her will
> We beseech Thee to hear us ...

And so on. All very wry and dry, if a bit overwrought in places. Slack strung, Heaney called this Kavanagh poem, but praised its "grim truth to life and gleeful language." His own spectral "crowd of shawled women", "wading the young corn", who appear in a ghostly throng to the accompaniment of bell-notes, create a more alluring, and also a more intense effect. They might be linked, via some common store of ancestral imagery, with "the girls in a noiseless procession / Going to Clachan as always" in Heaney's translation of Sorley MacLean's great poem "Hallaig" – or even, by a stretch, with the long-dead rustic dancers in Eliot's "East Coker".

The Carleton of "Station Island" has good advice for Seamus Heaney: "Remember everything and keep your head." He goes on: "We are earthworms of the earth, and all that / has gone through us is what will be our trace" – which may or may not refer back to the arresting image in the

Carleton "Lough Derg" story, which has the pilgrims of the day crawling slowly round the penitential beds "like worms on a dead dog." Section Two of "Station Island" ends with William Carleton, in his nineteenth-century overcoat and boots, fading out of the picture and making way — somewhat in the manner of the old-time Christmas Rhymers recalled by John Hewitt ("Here comes I, wee Devil Doubt") — making way for the next instructional revenant, or "fosterer" (Patrick Kavanagh, briefly). The lines describing Carleton's exit — "He turned on his heel as he was saying this / and started up the road at the same hard pace" — these lines chime very closely with the final lines of Section Five of "Little Gidding", which go as follows:

> ... in the disfigured street
> He left me, with a kind of valediction,
> And faded on the blowing of the horn

— "he", as we know, having crystallised by this stage into the shade of W.B. Yeats. Readers slightly bothered by the exclusion of Yeats from Heaney's "Station Island" were put right by the poet: Yeats could not have been part of the cast, he said, "because, to put it crudely, the pilgrimage was for Papists." So, instead, here comes I, James Joyce — ex-Papist and no pilgrimage aficionado — moving centre stage in the final section, to speak out with distinctiveness and authority:

> let others wear the sackcloth and the ashes.
> Let go, let fly, forget.
> You've listened long enough. Now strike your note.

We, engrossed readers, can now see Heaney's Lough Derg pilgrimage as a device for formulating a declaration of intent — as well as being a rich interfusion of evocation, individuality and authenticity. But just to return for a moment to the absence of W.B. Yeats. Non-Papist or not, Yeats could in fact have been smuggled into "Station Island" on the strength of a single late poem called "The Pilgrim", which is cast in a very jaunty mode: "Round Lough Derg's holy island I went upon the stones, / I prayed at all the stations upon my marrow-bones ..." This Yeats poem contains the intriguing observation, "All know that all the dead in the world about that place are stuck": all the dead in the world, alas, now including Seamus Heaney himself — whose shade may perhaps be invoked by some future secular pilgrim-poet or seeker-after-truth. But Heaney should have the last word here himself, and here it is – not from "Station Island" but from one of his final, as-yet-uncollected poems, "In a Field". This poignant work harks back to the First World War, to Edward Thomas, and to a Cork relation-by-marriage in the British Army who arrived one day at the Mossbawn farm in south County Derry (before Seamus was born). Heaney envisages this [dead] person taking

> me by a hand to lead me back
> Through the same old gate into the yard
> Where everyone has suddenly appeared.
>
> All standing waiting.

This essay was first delivered as a plenary address at "Seamus Heaney: A Conference and a Commemoration", Queen's University Belfast, on 13 April 2014.

A critic, essayist and anthologist, Patricia Craig was born and grew up in Belfast, and lived for many years in London before returning to Northern Ireland in 1999. She has written biographies of Elizabeth Bowen and Brian Moore, and edited many anthologies including The Oxford Book of Ireland, English Detective Stories, Modern Women's Stories, The Belfast Anthology *and* The Ulster Anthology. *Her memoir* Asking for Trouble *(Blackstaff Press) was published in 2007. She is a regular contributor to* The Irish Times, The Independent *and the* Times Literary Supplement.

THREE POEMS

—

Moya Cannon

BILBERRY BLOSSOM ON SEEFIN
For J

Half-way between mist and cloud,
we saw it by the barbed-wire fence –
pink-edged boxwood,
and the flowers, rosy cats' bells,
so round and waxy, we took them for berries,
but May is too early –
and after that there were low clumps everywhere,
the tiny bells secretive as nipples.
It bloomed through last years' heather
up near the summit,
where we unwrapped our sandwiches
as wind sheared through an empty tomb.

I imagined the bilberry-pickers
who used to climb the hills in August,
the long-dead boys and girls –
cattle-herders, butter-makers,
singers, dancers – brash and shy
as any disco- or club-goer
and full of the tug of summer's long desire.

And on our way down, just across the path
from a storm-flayed swatch of pine
grew great clumps of the pink and green bushes.

And later still,
as we drove down the mountain road
they grew tall along the verge,
so we pulled in and picked big bunches

to carry home
all the ringing promise
of that blossom and leaf
which we had often seen before
but had never heard.

ALICE LICHT

Three shoe brushes in a museum case,
the kind of brushes whose soft swish
I used hear every morning –
my father "feeding the leather"
of his creased brown shoes.

The Reich needs brushes, the half-blind
Otto Weidt insisted, thumping the table
of a Berlin police station
and I need my Jews to make them.
Give me back my Jews.

With the help of his ally,
the policeman,
he got them back,
those blind and deaf Jews
and some he pretended were blind and deaf.
He led them back in a long line,
like children holding hands,
like children released
from a door in the mountainside,
to Rosenthaler St,
where they worked for two years more
making brushes, binding brooms,
in his small, factory in the *höfe*
with its narrow rooms
painted with pink and green borders,
with its windowless room at the end
where he hid a Jewish family.

And once, he drove in his car
to the gates of Auschwitz "to sell brushes" —
as if any brush could clean a hell-floor —
his purpose being to carry back
three Jews, a young woman, Alice Licht
and her parents.
In the transport from Theresienstadt,
through the wooden floor slats,
she had posted a card to him,
signing herself "Alice Worry".

The parents died
as did, in the end,
in spite of Otto's ruses and bribes,
all the blind and deaf brush-makers.
They were swept up one morning
late in the war,
by men in shining boots.

His message was passed to Alice Licht
and she, at last,
escaped to Berlin,
stood at his window
as the war ended,
a small light,
like courage,
or blind hope.

THE COLLAR

In the corner of the vast, captured mosque
of Abd al-Rahman —
a spreading forest
of salvaged Roman pillars, Arab arches,
and a cathedral like a perched stork —
in the cordial city, where for a time,
Muslims, Christians and Jews lived

and worked in amity,
above the locked iron gates of a chapel,
dedicated to the Virgin Mary,
we saw a small, dusty, medallion,
containing a castellated coat of arms,
the inscription *Ave Maria, Gratia Plena*,
and a turbaned moor,
chained in an iron collar.

And the mosque –
began to fill up
with the clatter of crusades,
the aroma of the baked crescents of Vienna,
the stink of the mass graves of Srebrenica
the dust of the toppled towers of New York,
the hum of drones over Pakistan,
the clank of that collar-chain
and the weeping of all those who were chained
and who chained in turn –

many victories,
many collars,
little grace.

Córdoba 2013

Moya Cannon was born in Dunfanaghy, Co Donegal, and now lives in Galway. Her fourth collection of poems, Hands, *was published by Carcanet Press in 2011. She is a member of Aosdána.*

TWO POEMS

—

Harry Clifton

FAROES

1

Beauty, boredom, black despair –
And the getting there

So easy, in my own head,
For I know it already,

Always have. The ocean music
Old as time, the north Atlantic

Sheepfolk, and the yarns they spin …
Tell me a story, then.

2

A little boy is lowered in a basket
To a clutch of gannet's eggs, a thousand feet
Above nothingness – *nice image* –

When the cliff-face, in a blinding storm of wingbeats,
Explodes outwards – *why the disappointment?* –
Dies away, across half a lifetime,

Sky and passing clouds, a higher education
Making time as it goes. *Let me decide* –
For you the image, for me the interpretations.

It is a small place, God knows. Small and ingrown,
Ocean all around it. Myth,
Not history, is the governing principle,

Nature more than myth. Imagine what family life
And politics, swathed in Atlantic mist
For weeks on end, must be in such a place —

So he went away. So yes, he went away,
And many years had to pass — *the rest of the world
Is another story* — before that night

He stood again, by the rumble of the ice-plant,
Smelling the fish-nets, curing-sheds
Of his native quay, the Sound between the mountains

Loud with the calvings of bergs and the bark of seals,
Old rope at his feet, old severed knots, loose ends —
And needless to say, no friends.

3

I am saying all this,
My dear, not to bore you,
A born islander, classic Faroese,
Gold hair, blue eyes

And a wonderful listening air
Beyond your years. I am,
As you will have gathered,
Deeply unhappy. Stratagems,

Evasions, are my second nature,
Never where I really am.
But those bright irradiations
Of beauty and calm,

Your white arms crossed
On the table, cradling your breasts,
Stream into me ... *Please do not ask*
Any more of the situation

Than it has to give.
Revisit my dreams, though.
Help me, at least, to live
In the great Gulf Stream

Of wind and tide, grey weather
That brings us together.
I know, as you play with your cup,
My time is up —

By now, you have got my drift,
My island, and my bearings.
I have never been near the Faroes.
No, you have never left.

NAFOOEY

> *... the hiding-places of my power*
> *Seem open; I approach, and then they close*
> (William Wordsworth, "Prelude")

We fished all day, caught nothing. You were wise
Uncle Michael, dead so long ago,
With your one specimen trout, a nine-pound *ferox*
Trolled from the depths along Maumtrasna Bay,
To give up there and then.

                            For the rest, gold weather,
Silhouettes. The boatman resting, Daddy
With a coronet of flies around his hatband,
Casting into the channel — nothing happening
But that vastness, that magnificence

All around me, entering my soul
Before I knew it. Cattle at the water,
Clattering in the shallows. The clink of a milk-can
Carrying, and the sound of a human voice,
In flat calm weather, on the tympanum
Of innocent hearing. Near and yet too far,
The big mystery, shunted into earshot,
And the long perspective into the Partry hills
That would darken slowly, on the long row home
To Ferry Bridge, and the fee for the boatman.

That, already, was a kind of death.
Past midnight, driving deeper
Into the mountains, through the twistedness of Finny,
The turfcutters' bridge, where the fish would rest
On their swim to Lough Nafooey and its greedy pike,
Its perch fry waiting to gorge themselves
On trout-spawn. Did the Hand that introduced them
Introduce evil into the universe,
Dream Nafooey? Dad had tried it once,
Got nothing, where a summer trickle entered
From the Devilsmother. It was down there somewhere
Deep in its depression, the length of it
Unseen, but weirdly felt. Poor Uncle Michael,
Daddy said, but now he is in Heaven,
And yes, I believed it.
                              For I had seen Heaven,
Felt Hell. But a day would come, returning
To that very place, when the dark would dissipate,
The bridge be just a bridge, the river a river,
The lough a ripple of innocuous water
On weedy stones, and the sea an hour to the west.

Harry Clifton was born in Dublin in 1952 and has travelled widely in Africa, Asia and Europe. He is the author of seven collections of poems, most recently Secular Eden: Paris Notebooks 1994–2004 *(Wake Forest University Press, 2007), and two prose publications. He was the Ireland Chair of Poetry between 2010 and 2013, and continues to live in Dublin.*

TWO FUNERALS

Paul Maddern

*On the occasion of the first annual
Heaney O'Driscoll Memorial Lecture.*

When Seamus Heaney died at the end of August last year the nation, and beyond, mourned. When Dennis O'Driscoll died the previous December, Seamus Heaney mourned – along with the thousands who knew and loved Dennis. A visibly shaken Seamus delivered the eulogy at Dennis's funeral, and he was there to watch as an honour-guard of poets lined the path to Dennis's final resting place.

Both funerals were immensely moving affairs, largely because of the shared sorrow but also, in part, because of the expression of belief in, and love of, poetry. On these occasions, Auden was proved wrong: poetry does make things happen.

When deciding how the John Hewitt Society might mark the passing of Seamus Heaney, a patron of the society, the committee was also keen to acknowledge the passing of Dennis, another great supporter. Many here today will know far better than me just how close the two men were – both on a personal level and in terms of sharing an intellectual, aesthetic and moral integrity. Seamus Heaney's collection of prose pieces and criticisms, *Finders Keepers*, is dedicated to Dennis O'Driscoll and his wife, Julie O'Callaghan. And it was Dennis O'Driscoll with whom Seamus Heaney agreed to co-operate in what will amount to the Nobel laureate's only autobiography, *Stepping Stones* – a series of insightful questions posed by Dennis to which Seamus responded with his typical mix of intelligence, candour and grace. The John Hewitt Committee hope both men and their respective families would be happy to see the friends paired together again in this series of talks.

The only suggestion the committee proposes to would-be speakers is that the talk address some aspect of the creative impulse. When thinking of who we might ask to deliver the first talk … well, it didn't take much thought. If we think of Seamus as published by Faber and Dennis by Anvil, we do them and Peter Fallon a disservice. Gallery Press has played an important role in both writers' publishing histories. Heaney's Gallery publications include *The Midnight Verdict*, *Crediting Poetry* (The Nobel Lecture, 1995), a co-translation of *Laments* by Jan Kochanowski, *The Last Walk* (translations from the Italian of Giovanni Pascoli, 2013) and *Spelling it Out* – an essay to honour his great friend and playwright, Brian Friel. And Gallery has produced two collections of Dennis's essays and critical works: *Troubled Thoughts, Majestic Dreams* (2001) and almost a year to the day he died, *The Outnumbered Poet* – which is a Poetry Book Society recommendation. But as important as their publishing connection with Gallery was their personal relationship with Peter. This connection is clear and proud in Dennis's writings, and so close was Peter to Seamus that he was there at the first major health scare, at the very end, and he read Seamus's beautiful poem "The Given Note" at the great man's funeral.

In his essay, "Peter Fallon Revisited" republished in *The Outnumbered Poet*, Dennis wrote:

> Peter Fallon was my first poet – the first I met, the first I heard read poems in public [...] Ringleader of every worthwhile poetry plot, he was rejuvenating and regenerating the art, dusting it off, stirring it up with the whirlwind stamina of a young Yeats or Pound. [...] And he remains for me what then he was. Poet first and foremost. Editor. Man on a sacred mission: passionate, driven, resolute. // Peter's energising omnipresence lit a neon torch for a generation that had had its fill of staidness and was hungry for an Irish poetry with more pizazz, more jizz, more jazz, one likelier to appeal to the metal-head music fan than the egghead academic.

Writing of a different but similarly significant mentor, Philip Hobsbaum, Seamus had this to say, and I'd like to think it applies, equally, to both Seamus and Dennis. Heaney wrote:

> I remember Hobsbaum's hospitality and encouragement with the special gratitude we reserve for those who have led us towards confidence in ourselves.

Dennis was the exemplar, par excellence, of this encouragement and so too by example, Seamus undoubtedly led readers and writers to have confidence in themselves and their identities. These qualities are embodied, too, in Peter Fallon, and it is with great pleasure the John Hewitt

Committee invites Peter Fallon to deliver the first Heaney O'Driscoll Memorial Lecture.

———

I want to close with a quote from Dennis. When thinking of why poetry matters, he wrote:

> Since words are spoken by everyone, the custody of language is a sufficient responsibility in itself for a poet. To inscribe in language some hitherto unexpressed area of experience – to fill in some blank corner of the human canvas – is worthwhile; to speak the small truths that feed into the bigger Truth. Also, the aspiration of poetry is always towards the creation of something permanent in language: in our era of the disposable, the ephemeral, this is counter-cultural – as, indeed, is the fact that genuine poetry transcends the blinkered vision of the journalistic present; it inhabits the present, but it is also very much in dialogue with the inherited forms and the great voices of the past.

If Dennis and Seamus are now part of our collective past, at the same time, as Peter has so ably demonstrated today, their work keeps them very much in the present.

The bulk of the above remarks were delivered before the first annual Heaney O'Driscoll Memorial Lecture, by Peter Fallon, on 28 August 2014 at the John Hewitt International Summer School, Market Place Theatre, Armagh. The concluding paragraph followed the Lecture.

Paul Maddern was born in Bermuda in 1962. He studied at Queen's University, Ontario and Queen's University Belfast. His first collection of poems, The Beachcomber's Report, *was published by Templar in 2010. He has taught creative writing at Queen's University Belfast and Leeds University. He currently lives in Groomsport, Co Down.*

SEAMUS HEANEY'S BEAUTY
(Eulogy)

Paul Muldoon

In Donnybrook.

I called the Heaney house once years ago. Maybe thirty years, now. The phone was answered by one of the boys. Michael, I'm pretty sure. He was a teenager at the time. Having known him since he was a kid, I was glad to have a chance to have a chat and hear what he was up to. After a while, Michael ventured, "I suppose you'll want to speak to head-the-ball?" Not being a parent at the time, I was a little taken aback by the familiarity, perhaps even the over-familiarity, of this nomenclature. Even if Michael didn't call Seamus "head-the-ball" to his face (which I'm pretty sure he didn't), I realize now that it was a very telling moment. It was a moment that suggested a wonderfully relaxed attitude between father and teenage son, one I now see as highly difficult to establish and maintain.

The Seamus Heaney who was renowned the world over was never a man who took himself too seriously, certainly not with his family and friends. He had, after all, a signal ability to make each of us feel connected not only to him but to one another. We've all spent many years thinking about his poetry. We'll all spend many more years thinking about it. It's the person rather than the poet I'm focussing on today. The person who did everything *con brio*, "with vigor." This was, after all, the Seamus Heaney who repurposed Yeats's description of a bronze chariot in his poem "Who Goes With Fergus?" and referred to his BMW as a "brazen car." However the Seamus Heaney we're here to celebrate today might be described, "brazen" is hardly a word that comes to mind. Anything that smacks of ostentation would be quite inappropriate. As would anything that smacks of meanness of spirit. A word that might come to mind is "bounteous". And, while I'm in the realm of the "B"s, maybe even "bouncy".

This last may seem a bit strange, but I have a distinct memory of playing football with Seamus, Michael and Christopher somewhere in or around Glanmore. When I say "football", I need to be clear, particularly when this could well have been in an era when soccer was perceived as a foreign game. Let's put it like this. It was not a game in which Seamus's talent for heading the ball was ever called on. It was Gaelic football, and I have to tell you that I speak as someone who's been shoulder-charged by Seamus Heaney. He bounced me off like snow off a plough. Benignly, though. "Benign" is another word that comes to mind.

Actually, "benign" is somewhat inadequate. "Big-hearted" is coming closer. On the subject of the heart, when Seamus was fitted with a monitored electronic device a few years ago he took an almost unseemly delight in announcing, "Blessed are the pacemakers." Seamus's big-hearted celebrity attracted other celebrities, of course. Movers and shakers always attract movers and shakers. Was it a young Michael (or a young Christopher, perhaps?) who was introduced to a couple of dinner guests and inquired of each of them in turn, "What is it you're famous for?" To return to Seamus's capacity to act *con brio*, I don't think I've ever seen another human being, with the possible exception of Usain Bolt, move with such speed and accuracy as did Seamus when he heard the then-toddler Catherine-Ann cry out in distress after falling in the yard. He positively sprinted, swept her up in his arms, brought her to a safe place.

It was Seamus Heaney's unparalleled capacity to sweep all of us up in his arms that we're honoring today. Though Seamus helped all of us develop our imaginative powers we can only imperfectly imagine what Marie is going through. She above all recognizes that other great attribute of Seamus Heaney. I'm thinking of his beauty. Today we mourn with Marie and the children, as well as the extended families, the nation, the wide world. We remember the beauty of Seamus Heaney — as a bard, and in his being.

Seamus Heaney's funeral took place at the Sacred Heart Church, Donnybrook, Dublin on 2 September 2013, before interment at Bellaghy Cemetery, Belllaghy, Co Derry later in the day. A second eulogy of Seamus as a husband and father was delivered at the end of the service by his son, Michael Heaney.

Paul Muldoon grew up in The Moy, Co Armagh. His most recent volume of poems is The Word on the Street *(Farrar, Strauss and Giroux, 2013). He is currently Howard G. B. Clark '21 Professor in the Humanities at Princeton University, and the Poetry Editor of* The New Yorker.

IN MEMORIAM SEAMUS HEANEY

A suite of obituaries.

IMMEASURABLY ENRICHED

Patricia Craig

Incredible staying power.

Seamus Heaney, who has died in hospital in Dublin at the age of 74 after a short illness, was probably the best-known poet in the world. He is irreplaceable, and for his many friends and admirers there will be a tremendous sense of private as well as public bereavement.

In his Nobel Prize acceptance speech, delivered in Stockholm in 1995, Heaney recalled his first encounter with European languages via the radio in the kitchen of his wartime Co Derry home. Overhearing fragments of foreign sentences, he said, as the dial was moved from one accustomed station to another, "I had already begun a journey into the wideness of the world. This in turn became a journey into the wideness of language, a journey where each point of arrival – whether in one's poetry or one's life – turned out to be a stepping stone rather than a destination, and it is that journey which has brought me now to this honoured spot."

In the same speech, with his customary felicity, Heaney paid tribute to his great predecessor W.B. Yeats, with whom he had inevitably been compared as far back as the 1970s, when his astonishing career was just beginning to get into its stride. His fourth collection, *North* (1975), was a stepping stone on the way to his ultimate status as the "greatest living poet" – the most widely read poet in English, possessor of incomparable gifts and impeccable instincts, and all the other superlatives heaped on him.

North was held by some to denote an artistic breakthrough, embodying as it did a new strength and sophistication following on from the pared-down, rural, evocations and intensities of the earlier collections. In Heaney's native Northern Ireland, though, its reception was less than adulatory. There were complicated reasons for this: for example, the "famous Seamus" brouhaha, which was starting up around this time, made a contrary assessment inevitable in the poet's home territory. More seriously, with the Troubles entering a horrific phase, it was felt that certain poems in the collection could be read as an endorsement of republicanism, with Heaney displaying, at best, as one critic wrote, "a culpable ambiguity in [his] responses to atrocity." Such reservations were, I think, based on a misreading; Heaney was never an apologist for violence, despite the seeming drift of the much-quoted lines about "conniving" in civilized outrage, while understanding "the exact / and tribal, intimate revenge." His brief was large enough to accord a right of expression to every variety of belief. And if "the dark matter of the news headlines" got into Heaney's poetry, as it did at intervals from this time on – though always contained within an oblique and subtle, multi-layered and illuminating, modus operandi – the light he was aiming for, he said, "was the kind that derives from clarity of expression, from plain speaking."

In any case, the voices of dissent soon died away as Heaney's place in the canon of contemporary literature became unassailable. The list of his honours is breathtaking, from the Cholmondeley Award for *Death of a Naturalist* onwards, culminating in the Nobel Laureateship. Professor of Poetry at Oxford University, Boylston Professor of Rhetoric and Oratory at Harvard, Emerson Poet in Residence, also at Harvard, Duff Cooper Memorial Award, American-Irish Foundation Award, Member of Aosdána and the Royal Irish Academy; few available honours, national or international, passed him by.

Nothing about Seamus Heaney's early life suggested the heights to which he would eventually rise. He was born in April 1939 at Mossbawn, near Castledawson in Co Derry, a remote corner of a remote part of Northern Ireland, symbolically placed, he said, "between the marks of English influence and the lure of the native experience, between the 'demesne' and the 'bog'." The first of nine children of a farmer and cattle dealer, Patrick Heaney, and his wife Margaret (*née* McCann), Heaney grew up surrounded by siblings and relations, friends and neighbours ("All of us there"), and immersed in the rituals of rural Catholic life.

> I come from scraggy farm and moss,
> Old patchworks that the pitch and toss
> Of history have left dishevelled ....

It was a happy childhood, and immensely fruitful for his future as a poet; but at 11 he began the journey that would separate him from country concerns and, in a sense, from the rest of his family. From Anahorish Primary School he passed the 11-plus and left on a scholarship to board during term time at St Columb's College in Derry city. (Other St Columb's pupils at the time included the future politician John Hume, and Heaney's friend and fellow poet Seamus Deane.)

From St Columb's, Heaney went on to Queen's University Belfast, and graduated with first-class honours in English in 1961. After completing a teacher-training course he obtained a post at St Thomas's Boys' School, where the novelist and short-story writer Michael McLaverty was headmaster. McLaverty was an early influence – "… to hell with overstating it", he warned, as recorded in the Heaney poem "Fosterage". At the same time the writers' workshop in Belfast set up and run by Philip Hobsbaum (then a lecturer at Queen's) provided further support and encouragement. Other members, or occasional participants in the Hobsbaum Group's activities included Michael and Edna Longley, Bernard MacLaverty, Joan Newmann, Stewart Parker, James Simmons and others; and beyond the Group a network of literary and artistic friendships was evolving, and Heaney established lifelong ties with fellow poets such as Michael Longley, Derek Mahon and John Montague (the irreverent *Honest Ulsterman* magazine described Heaney, Mahon and Longley as "the tight-arsed trio" due to their preference for a formal, rather than an experimental, approach).

Predecessors such as Patrick Kavanagh in particular, but also Louis MacNeice and John Hewitt, indicated a way forward – no more – for the Heaney *oeuvre*, while a handful of English poets from Wordsworth to Ted Hughes contributed something to its development. Other kindred spirits of Heaney's, around this time and for the future, were the painters Colin Middleton and T.P. Flanagan, and the great folk singer and "free spirit" David Hammond. After some years in the doldrums, Belfast in the early 1960s was shaping up for something of a cultural efflorescence.

In 1965 Heaney married Marie Devlin from Ardboe, near Toome (one of six clever and beautiful sisters who included the author Polly Devlin), and the couple's first son was born the following year. That year his first collection, *Death of a Naturalist*, was published by Faber and Faber; and he was appointed to the staff of Queen's University as a lecturer in English. *Door into the Dark* came out in 1969, followed by *Wintering Out* three years later. By this stage it was clear that something unusual was happening in the field of contemporary poetry: Heaney, according a critic in *Punch*, "writes with the authority of a man who has his own vision of the world", while the

Guardian wrote that he "has the gift of finding a new and consummate phrase to evoke physical qualities ... the result is superb"; for the *Observer*, he "has already left the point at which his contemporaries are now arriving." A year as Visiting Professor at the University of California, Berkeley, helped to broaden his outlook. "Something changed, all right", he told Dennis O'Driscoll in 2007. "It had to do with the intellectual distinction of the people around us, the nurture that came from new friendships and a vivid environment."

When the Berkeley year was over, Heaney returned with his family (a second son had been born in 1968) to Northern Ireland and a state of escalating Troubles. Internment had just been introduced; five months later came the Bloody Sunday shootings in Derry and then the Bloody Friday bombings in Belfast. The Heaneys had been contemplating a move for some time and in 1972, Heaney having resigned his post at Queen's, they left Belfast for Wicklow, where they rented a cottage at Glanmore from the Synge scholar Ann Saddlemyer – "Belfast was where we grew up", Heaney said. "In Glanmore we were grown-ups when we arrived." Around this time, Heaney was consolidating literary friendships with Robert Lowell, Ted Hughes and Joseph Brodsky, among others. He had also, through his teaching at Queen's, got to know some Irish poets of a slightly younger generation, among them Paul Muldoon, Frank Ormsby, Ciaran Carson, Medbh McGuckian. For these, he was already something of an exemplar.

North was published in 1975, with the famous "bog" poems inspired by PV Glob's book *The Bog People* (though the first of these had appeared in the previous collection, *Wintering Out*). Heaney had returned to teaching, at Carysfort College of Education in Dublin, where he continued until 1981; in the meantime, *Field Work* (1979) and *Preoccupations: Selected Prose 1968–78* (1980) had come out, to great acclaim: "deliberate ... restrained ... authoritative and universal", Harold Bloom wrote of the former in the *TLS*. "Wry, spare, compressed, subtle, strange" was the verdict of Richard Ellmann. By now, for part of the year, Heaney was engaged as a visiting lecturer at Harvard, and revelling in the acquaintance of new colleagues such as Helen Vendler (to whom his book *The Spirit Level* is dedicated) and Elizabeth Bishop.

There were many trips abroad, to the US, to Macedonia, Spain, Mexico, Rotterdam, Scotland, France and Japan, but at this time (the late 1970s) the Heaney family was based in Dublin, at Sandymount, a move undertaken partly to facilitate their children's schooling (a daughter, Catherine Ann, was born in 1973), though they kept on the Glanmore cottage and eventually bought it from Anne Saddlemyer. For Heaney, Glanmore was, and remained, a place of refuge, a writing retreat, somewhere he could escape from the obligations and disruptions consequent on extreme celebrity. Heaney was incessantly in demand, for book launches, exhibition openings, broadcasts, films, lectures, endorsements of this or that enterprise or publication, and his nature made it difficult for him to refuse whatever was asked of him. The pressure was enormous, and his wife Marie had sometimes to intervene to save him from the effects of his instinctive obligingness. His daily post arrived at the house in sackfuls, and consisted mainly of requests, all of which he was loth to decline. It was a matter of courtesy, of a strong sense of the other person's feelings. When his friend Karl Miller asked him if he was really as nice as he seemed, Heaney replied wryly that he had been "cursed with a fairly decent set of impulses."

It was a busy life, requiring tremendous energy and dedication. Whatever public obligations he fulfilled, though – and they were innumerable – Heaney always made time for his family and his many friends, and for his own work (which was, indeed, the cause of the international reputation which made him a prime target for besiegers of all kinds, whose importunings would have stopped him from getting on with it). The books continued to appear: *Station Island* (1984), which, according to John Carey in the *Sunday Times*, surpassed "even what one might expect from this magnificently gifted poet"; *The Haw Lantern* (1987); *Seeing Things* (1991); *The Spirit Level* (1996); *Electric Light* (2001). There were also prose collections, translations, and two anthologies, *The Rattle Bag* and *The School Bag*, edited with Ted Hughes.

On top of all this, Heaney was a director of the Field Day Theatre Company (founded by Brian Friel and Stephen Rea), under whose auspices *The Cure at Troy*, a version of Sophocles' *Philoctetes*, was premiered in 1990. Then came the Nobel Prize for Literature in 1995, and the attendant to-do, after which demands on his time and stamina entered an even more exorbitant phase. It didn't affect his output, though. His translation of *Beowulf* (1999) won the Whitbread Book of the Year award. As Karl Miller (again) observed: "Seamus Heaney believes in keeping going. He has a poem in which a brother does this [his brother Hugh, in the poem of that title from *The Spirit Level*], and he has done it himself." Incredible staying power was a Heaney characteristic.

So too was the power of recovery. All this, the activity overload, took its toll; and in 2006, while staying in a guesthouse in Donegal to attend a friend's birthday party, Heaney suffered a mild stroke. It was the year his eleventh collection, *District and Circle*, had been published; the poem "Anything Can Happen", an adaptation of one of Horace's odes and obliquely referring to the Twin Towers attacks, might be read, with hindsight, as anticipating the poet's illness, which came out of the blue and skewed his perception of the world for a time. He was quickly transferred by ambulance to a hospital in Dublin and spent the next five weeks reading detective novels and coming to terms with what had happened. (One of his earliest visitors was Bill Clinton, the former US president.) He pulled through, as it seemed, without lasting ill effects, though his doctors instructed him to eschew all public commitments for at least a year. Ever humorous, "the rest cure" was how Heaney described his stay in hospital. And as soon as the year was up he resumed his life of plentiful public engagements. His last appearance was at the Merriman Summer School in Lisdoonvarna, Co Clare, on 16 August; there, he and his friend and fellow poet Michael Longley gave a joint reading, to vast applause.

The year following his stroke, however, saw Heaney immersed in a new and different project. *Stepping Stones*, a series of extensive interviews with him conducted by fellow poet Dennis O'Driscoll, was published in 2008. Heaney, at 68, was in a position to take stock, to reflect on the past and all its implications. As in the poem "Aerodrome", it was a case of

Bearings taken, markings, cardinal points,
Options, obstinacies, dug heels and distance,
Here and there and now and then, a stance.

Prompted by a thoughtful and intrepid interlocutor, Heaney came up with extraordinarily lucid, compelling and forthright answers to questions about his life and times, attitudes and angles of vision. Not an exercise in self-revelation, or a quasi-autobiography, *Stepping Stones* is rather a guideline to crucial events in its subject's life, in both the public and the personal sphere (though the private core remained private, a necessary counterbalance to all the celebrated Heaney geniality and public acclaim). What shines through these interviews is the sense of a person of unprecedented gifts and equally rare integrity, as a poet, husband, father, friend and "mythologized public figure."

When Heaney's twelfth collection, *Human Chain*, came out in 2010, Peter McDonald, writing in the *TLS*, hailed it as a work which "allows questions of death and rebirth, forgetting and memory, and parents and children, to set an agenda which the poems themselves both address and transform." The same reviewer noted the book's engagement with the *Aeneid*, the Virgilian underworld, though, as he said, the poems are located "every bit as firmly in County Derry." It is a pertinent observation: throughout his life Heaney remained true to his origins, to his experiences as part of a minority existing uneasily in the north of Ireland under unionist rule. Nothing about his attitude was ever inflexible, though. During the Queen's state visit to Ireland in 2010, Heaney was placed next to her at a formal dinner, despite the lines from "An Open Letter" asserting his Irish identity: "No glass of ours was ever raised / To toast the Queen." He remained true to the concept of neighbourliness transcending sectarian imperatives, to the forked hazel-stick, the lamps swung though the yards on winter evenings, the cairns and drains and outlying fields and the sandstone coping of Anahorish Bridge. He forgot nothing, and took it all in. Because of him, the worlds of his childhood, of his exemplary life, of Northern Ireland, of literature in general, are immeasurably enriched. "And afterwards, rust, thistles, silence, sky."

This obituary was first published in The Independent *on 31 August 2014.*

A critic, essayist and anthologist, Patricia Craig was born and grew up in Belfast, and lived for many years in London before returning to Northern Ireland in 1999. She has written biographies of Elizabeth Bowen and Brian Moore, and edited many anthologies including The Oxford Book of Ireland, English Detective Stories, Modern Women's Stories, The Belfast Anthology *and* The Ulster Anthology. *Her memoir* Asking for Trouble *(Blackstaff Press) was published in 2007. She is a regular contributor to* The Irish Times, The Independent *and the* Times Literary Supplement.

——

A LUMINOUS EMPTINESS

Roy Foster

Abundant personality.

My first thought on hearing the immeasurably sad news of Seamus Heaney's death was a sensation of a great tree having fallen: that sense of empty space, desolation, uprooting. Heaney's place in Irish culture – not just in Irish poetry – was often compared to that of W.B. Yeats, particularly after he followed Yeats in winning the Nobel Prize in 1995. He possessed what he himself ascribed to Yeats, "the gift of establishing authority within a culture." But whereas Yeats's shadow was seen, by some of his younger contemporaries at least, as blotting out the sun and stunting the growth of the surrounding forest, Heaney's great presence let in the light. Part of this was bound up in his own abundant personality. Generosity, amplitude and sympathy characterized his dealings with people at every level, and he was the stellar best of company. It was as if he had learned the lesson prescribed (though not really followed) by Yeats: that the creative soul, "all hatred driven hence", might recover "radical innocence" in being "self-delighting, self-appeasing, self-affrighting."

But behind the marvellous manner, unforced charm and wicked hoots of laughter he was one of the most formidable critical intellects of his day, a powerfully subtle analyst of political and social nuance, and the possessor of intellectual antennae that let nothing past them. Living in Ireland and being world famous was not an unmixed blessing – he described the effects of winning the Nobel as "a mostly benign avalanche" – and he knew how to elegantly evade the occasional begrudgery of others and withdraw into his own resources, sustained by a beloved family life. The distinctiveness of his poetry was unmistakable: a Heaney poem carried its maker's mark on the blade. So was the immense labour that went into the deceptive simplicity of his early collections (throughout his writing career he drew terrific metaphors and images from an extraordinary range of physical work practices). And part of the impact of that early work lay in his use of violence.

That this was often done by implication made it no less shocking; the authentic lifting of the hairs on the back of the neck that I still remember when I opened *North* (1975), with its exploration of the archaeology of atrocity, was replicated in reading *Station Island* (1984), with its extraordinary title poem tracing a ghostly Dantean journey through the shades of Irish history, meeting with the dead. This culminates in a visionary encounter with Joyce ("His voice eddying with the vowels of all rivers / came back to me, though he did not speak yet, / a voice like a prosecutor's or a singer's, / cunning, narcotic, mimic, definite"), and Joyce spoke to Heaney in more ways than one. Listening to him on *Desert Island Discs* some years ago, I waited for him to choose Yeats's poems as his elected book, only to hear him demand *Ulysses* instead; on reflection I was not surprised. His own capaciousness was Joycean.

Like Joyce, Heaney's erudition was immense, and his lectures on literature at Oxford, Harvard and worldwide made wonderful reading and unparalleled listening. They illustrate his openness to world literature and Classical history as well as his deep love of unexpected English poets such as Clare and Wordsworth — and his affinity with writers from eastern Europe, Osip Mandelstam above all. "There is an unsettled aspect to the different worlds they inhabit", he wrote in *The Government of the Tongue* (1988), "and one of the challenges they face is to survive amphibiously, in the realm of 'the times' and the realm of their moral and artistic self-respect." This carried — as he himself pointed out — a resonant echo for a poet afflicted by "the awful and demeaning facts of Northern Ireland's history." He lived in Dublin but never evaded those "facts" of his native territory. Indeed, part of Heaney's immense achievement was to use and expand that "awfulness" and its relation to the creative spirit and artistic commitment, using implication rather than assertion — whether in the haunting parallels and allegories of *North*, or in later poems like "From the Frontier of Writing" and "From the Republic of Conscience".

The note is there also in his wonderful last collection, *Human Chain* (2010), where one is pulled — yet again — in the wake of a writer able to push out the boat into a limitless sea. But what struck me most in reading it, along with the almost daunting economy of line, was a whispering sense of elegy — not just because many of the poems were dedicated to the dead, but also because they looped back to his earliest images of pen nibs, farm routines, animal life, the rituals of neighbourhood, and love. This sense of an ending was perhaps a sign of poetic prescience.

At the time of his death, though, I come back to the image of the death of a tree. I remember now that he wrote about this himself — both in a marvellous 1985 essay on the work of Patrick Kavanagh, and then in a sonnet sequence, "Clearances", in memory of his mother. The tree in question grew from a chestnut which his aunt planted in a jam jar in 1939, the year of Heaney's birth; it flourished, was transplanted to the garden, became a fully sized tree "that grew as I grew" and came to symbolize his own developing life – until, in his early teens, the family moved away from the house and the new owners cut it down. The absence of the tree then created in Heaney's mind "a kind of luminous emptiness." He now identified, he wrote, with "preparing to be unrooted, to be spirited away into some transparent, yet indigenous afterlife." This is the thought that he put into "Clearances" (whose final sonnet is below), and I think of it now as I remember the marvellous spirit of a great poet who was also a great man.

> I thought of walking round and round a space
> Utterly empty, utterly a source
> Where the decked chestnut tree had lost its place
> In our front hedge among the wallflowers.
> The white chips jumped and jumped and skited high.
> I heard the hatchet's differentiated
> Accurate cut, the crack, the sigh
> And collapse of what luxuriated
> Through the shocked tips and wreckage of it all.
> Deep-planted and long gone, my coeval
> Chestnut from a jam jar in a hole,
> Its heft and hush became a bright nowhere,
> A soul ramifying and forever
> Silent, beyond silence listened for.

This obituary was first published in The Guardian *on 1 September 2014.*

One of Ireland's most celebrated scholars, Roy Foster is Carroll Professor of Irish History at Hertford College, Oxford. His most recent book is Words Alone: Yeats and his Inheritances *(Oxford University Press, 2011).*

———

GOING GRATEFULLY

Neil Corcoran

Facing down the worst.

In 2009, as part of the extensive celebrations in Ireland for his seventieth birthday, RTÉ broadcast a documentary about Seamus Heaney. Towards its close, Heaney, who has died aged 74, was asked whether anything in his work seemed appropriate to him as an epitaph. He demurred at first but, when gently prodded, quoted what he had translated from *Oedipus at Colonus* by Sophocles when his friend the great Polish poet Czesław Miłosz died in 2004. Telling the story of the old king who dies and vanishes into the earth, the play's Messenger says, in Heaney's version: "Wherever that man went, he went gratefully." That, said Heaney, would do for him too.

The gratitude is not so much, surely, for the leaving of life, but for the work well done. Heaney suffered a stroke in 2006 and his volume *Human Chain* (2010) is painfully shadowed by ageing and mortality. But it is also deeply informed by a spirit of resilience and acceptance and, in the extraordinary love poem "Chanson d'Aventure", which describes his ambulance drive to hospital with his wife, Marie, by the sense of renewal and new reward, even at a late stage, in human relationships.

Mortality and domestic relations, affection and obligation, had preoccupied Heaney throughout his work, and were frequently sounded together. One of his most popular poems, "Mid-Term Break", from his collection *Death of a Naturalist* (1966), handles the death of his younger brother Christopher in a road accident in 1953, when Heaney was still a schoolboy; that loss is returned to again in the superb late poem "The Blackbird of Glanmore", in *District and Circle* (2006), which is also concerned with intimations of the poet's own mortality.

The deaths of many in the Troubles feature in numerous Heaney poems, notably in *North* (1975), where, in the now famous sequence of "bog poems", they are brought into alignment with the Iron-Age bodies recovered from the bogs of Jutland, which Heaney had encountered in P.V. Glob's book *The Bog People*. In the collections *Field Work* (1979) and *Station Island* (1984), Heaney encounters ghosts. With these poems, and others, he became one of the great modern elegists.

But Heaney was also an excellent poet of familial love and, notably, of enduring married love. There are numerous poems of filial affection, for both mother and father, and wonderful poems for his children and, latterly, his granddaughter. One of his finest poems, "Sunlight", in *North*, was written for his aunt Mary, who was partly responsible for his upbringing. "Chanson d'Aventure" marked a late stage in the marital relationship he had vividly portrayed for years after his marriage to Marie Devlin in 1965: from the difficulties evoked in "Summer Home" (in *Wintering Out*, 1972), a poem of regret and self-recrimination, through the stabilities, accommodations, supportiveness, sources of strength and erotic tenderness and arousal recorded in such poems as "The Skunk" and "An Afterwards in Field Work" (1979), and "The Underground" and "La Toilette" in *Station Island*.

Especially in its bleak treatment of the Troubles, Heaney's poetry is full of broken things, but it is also a poetry of the continuities that sustain us against mortality. His resourceful, disciplined equilibrium finds one of its best expressions at the end of "A Kite for Michael and Christopher", in *Station Island*, when the poet-father hands the emblematic kite on to his sons:

Before the kite plunges down into the wood
and this line goes useless
take in your two hands, boys, and feel
the strumming, rooted, long-tailed pull of grief.
You were born fit for it.
Stand in here in front of me
and take the strain.

The way his work faces the worst but steadies itself against it, too, must be the greatest single reason for Heaney's huge readership. He presumably had his popularity in mind when he called himself, in *Station Island*, a "poet, lucky poet."

The eldest of nine children of Margaret (*née* McCann) and Patrick Heaney, a Catholic farmer and cattle dealer, he was born at Mossbawn farm near the village of Castledawson in Co Derry. Seamus was an early beneficiary of the 1947 Northern Ireland Education Act, attending St Columb's College in Derry, where his contemporaries included the politician John Hume and the critic and academic Seamus Deane. He studied English language and literature at Queen's University Belfast, graduating with a first-class degree in 1961. He taught for a brief period in Belfast and joined the writers' workshop known as the Group, initiated by the poet and critic Philip Hobsbaum, who taught at Queen's. After Hobsbaum left the university, Heaney was appointed to a lectureship in English in 1966 and he became chairman of the Group, whose other members included Michael Longley and Bernard MacLaverty. An important impetus to the burgeoning of poetry in the north, it would eventually also include the poets Paul Muldoon, Medbh McGuckian and Ciaran Carson.

In 1964 Karl Miller published three of Heaney's poems in the *New Statesman*, where they were noticed by the Northern Irish-born Charles Monteith, one of the directors of the publishers Faber and Faber. When he received Monteith's letter soliciting a manuscript, it was, Heaney said, "like getting a letter from God the Father." Two years later, Faber published *Death of a Naturalist*. It received exceptional acclaim, and Heaney almost immediately became a poet keenly watched, followed and imitated. By then, he had married Devlin, with whom he would have three children, Michael, Christopher and Catherine Ann.

This obituary was first published in The Guardian *on 31 August 2014.*

Coda: A Brief Reminiscence after His Death

He gave me what he called "a sacramental drink." I recalled it as *poitín*, the Irish moonshine. Until, telling someone so years later, I wondered if it had been sloe gin; "bitter / and dependable", he calls it in the poem. There was theatre and twinkle in the way he said it, though, relaxing me and dissipating distance; but earnest too.

What I was seeing when he said *poitín*, if that is what he said, was Dingle years before when my father bought a salmon gaffed near Annascaul. A salmon for a pound, in 1963; the deal ratified in contraband from the garage below. Its tart and acrid stink is in my nostrils still: bitter, but scarcely yet dependable.

Neil Corcoran is Emeritus Professor of English at the University of Liverpool. The author of several books of literary criticism, his volume Seamus Heaney: A Critical Study *(Faber, 1986 & revised 1998) remains a seminal and unrivalled overview of the poet's work.*

MONUMENTS OF THE DREAM LIFE

Colm Tóibín

One eye on the door.

Two years ago I invited Seamus Heaney to read at the Kilkenny Arts Festival in Ireland. The venue was St Canice's Cathedral, one of the most beautiful churches in Ireland. It was here almost 40 years earlier that, as a young poet, he had met Robert Lowell, who had become a friend and a mentor. Heaney admired Lowell's utter dedication to his craft, his ability to change, his absolute belief in the importance of poetry. When I suggested that Dennis O'Driscoll, who had done a book of interviews with Heaney, should introduce him on stage, Seamus said he would like that, but he would prefer it if Dennis would read as well. Dennis, he said, had done enough introducing; since he was also a poet, he should get equal billing. It was typical of Seamus's generosity.

That evening, I suggested to him that he should do no signing of books after the reading, but go and have a drink with the theatre director Peter Brook, who was in Kilkenny and wanted to meet him. As we left by a side door and walked away from the church, he sighed and said that all his life after readings when everyone else was free to walk out into the world, he would spent an hour or more signing books and meeting people. He was the most tactful and careful and scrupulous of men. He used a deep-rooted conscientiousness in his work, but it also came across every time you met him. He had a way of holding back, watching every word, weighing the moment. In his public readings he had a real command; privately, he was almost shy, always thoughtful.

That summer's evening, I sensed that he was enjoying a sort of freedom which was apparent in his work after the volume *Seeing Things* in 1991. He played a seriousness and a responsibility against an urge to loosen his tone without slackening the care he took with every phrase; he felt easier about celebrating things, allowing the miraculous into his work and a sort of lightness into his cadences. At first he felt guilty about not staying behind to sign books and satisfy other people's needs, but then he smiled and walked with a casual stride, seeming to enjoy the dwindling summer light, the freedom, the prospect of good company.

He remained a northerner in the south of Ireland. Even though he lived in Wicklow and Dublin for 40 years, he was a citizen of south Derry and then of the world of poetry. What happened in the north weighed on him. In a time of burnings and bombings he used poetry to offer an alternative world; he gave example by his seriousness, his honesty, the tact in his phrasing, the care with language, the thoughtfulness, the scrupulousness.

He carried his fame lightly, easily. He preferred shadow to light; he preferred the half-said, careful, ambiguous remark to the big statement; he liked the slow smile rather than the easy laugh. He enjoyed company, but I always felt he had one eye on the door, and would be happy when the night was over and he could go home.

For his readers, his books were events in our lives, monuments. All of us remember reading the poems in *North*, say, for the first time in 1975, or reading the Glanmore sonnets which appeared in his book *FieldWork* in 1979. He was not merely a central figure in the literary life of Ireland, but in its emotional life, in its dream life, in its real life. In his last book, *Human Chain*, published in 2010, he wrote about growing older and weaker with a shivering honesty and grace. It is hard to come to terms now with the idea that there will be no more such books.

This obituary was first published in The Guardian *on 31 August 2014.*

One of Ireland's most celebrated verbal artists across all genres, Colm Tóibín is the author of ten works of fiction, most recently Nora Webster *(Viking, 2014).*

THE GREAT CITIZEN

Fintan O'Toole

It will play on in our heads.

Like all great poets, Seamus Heaney was an alchemist.

He turned our disgrace into grace, our petty hatreds into epic generosity, our dull clichés into questioning eloquence, the leaden metal of brutal inevitability into the gold of pure possibility.

He lacked the arrogance to tell us who we are – much more importantly, he told us what we are. He reminded us that Ireland is a culture before it is an economy. And in the extraordinary way he bore himself, the dignity and decency and the mellow delight that shone from him, he gave us self-respect.

In *The Tempest*, Miranda exclaims "O brave new world, / That has such people in it." Seamus Heaney made us gasp in wonder that, for all its follies and terrors, Irish culture had such a person in it.

He was out and about again this spring and summer, reading, opening, presiding, blessing. After he suffered a stroke in 2006, he had cut down on his public engagements, resisting the incessant clamour for his presence. But this year he seemed happy to be a public man again.

He had something to convey – especially, it seemed, to his fellow citizens. It was what his whole life as a poet had articulated with such astounding eloquence. In a speech at the National Museum in March he put it directly: "We are not simply a credit rating or an economy but a history and a culture, a human population rather than a statistical phenomenon."

No one did so much to make us feel like creatures of a long-working imagination rather than figments of a short-term market.

Great poets speak for themselves but they also create the voices through which something beyond themselves finds articulation. What Heaney articulated, above all, was the way in which – in the words of his friend Brian Friel – confusion need not be an ignoble condition. He grew up in a literally divided landscape – "the lines of sectarian antagonism and affiliation", he wrote, "followed the boundaries of the land" – and lived through the hopes and horrors of the Troubles.

He was drawn to both Irish and English poetic traditions. He also lived through the death of the ancient rural world into which he was born and the emergence of a globalized modern Ireland. He struggled with contradictions, paradoxes, conflicting impulses.

His genius lay in his ability to hover between them, to give each side of a political or emotional equation its full weight and proper due without becoming the prisoner of either. W.B. Yeats, the poet whose influence he both absorbed and transcended, wrote in a time of Irish violence that "we are closed in and the key is turned / On our uncertainty."

Heaney told us that, though we are indeed fated to uncertainty, it need not necessarily be a locked room in which we play out the same scenarios of doom over and over. Uncertainty may simply be the human condition.

Heaney humanized uncertainty, made ambiguity rich with possibilities. As he put it in the beautifully homely metaphor of "Terminus":

Two buckets were easier carried than one.
I grew up in between.

He was not, in that sense, a national poet. He knew too much about the dangers of tribalism and the foolishness of slogans to ever want to be a spokesman for the collective. He would have agreed with Yeats's dictum that "We make out of the quarrel with others, rhetoric, but of the quarrel with ourselves, poetry."

In Heaney's "The Flight Path", an IRA sympathizer has his demands for political commitment refused:

When, for fuck's sake, are you going to write
Something for us?
If I do write something,
Whatever it is, I'll be writing for myself.

But that self was never selfish. It was always open, sensitive, attuned to the signals emanating not just from nature and memory, but from politics and history too. With the outbreak of the Troubles, as he put it, "the problems of poetry moved from being simply a matter of achieving the satisfactory verbal icon to being a search for images and symbols adequate to our predicament." This was his lifelong quest – for images and symbols adequate to the predicament of being alive in his own time.

What forced him to be great, what kept him on his mettle, was that this quest was for him a very hard struggle. His world, the world of his childhood to which he returned so often and with such breathtaking clarity of recall, was archaic: farmers ploughing with horses, thatchers making roofs from rushes, diviners finding hidden sources of water, blacksmiths working in their forges. He could have lived imaginatively only in that world, as a nostalgic romantic, purveyor of hand-woven verbal tweeds. He fought instead to make his art contemporary, to put it under the pressure of its times.

He was often racked, indeed, by a sense that this art was in fact inadequate. The image of his cousin Colum McCartney, murdered in a sectarian attack, haunted him: "blood and roadside muck in your hair and eyes."

But he knew too that there was an immense human value in the act of writing with infinite care and utter honesty, in the way poetry acts as an antidote to the murderous clichés of slogans and rhetoric. Heaney recalled of himself and his fellow Belfast-based poets in the early 1960s that they were buoyed by a belief "that the tolerances and subtleties of their art were precisely what they had to set against the repetitive intolerance of public life."

That belief may have seemed naive in the bleakest years of the Troubles but in the longer perspective of history it was vindicated. It was not accidental that, when politicians reached for a language adequate to the unfolding of new possibilities for peace, they took Heaney's "hope and history rhyme" off the shelf again and again. The poet in Heaney was surely wearied by hearing his new-minted phrase worn away into cliché, but the citizen in him would have regarded the sacrifice as well worth making.

The great maker of such phrases will not be lost, for he is among the immortals now. But the great citizen, the exemplary public man who gave a gentle gravity to our small affairs, who blessed our ordinary days with intimations of the extraordinary, is a devastating loss to Irish life. We can take comfort where we will best find it: in his own luminous poems. There we will find a recurrent imagine of marks that have been erased in physical reality but go on existing.

He wrote of "the dotted line my father's ashplant made on Sandymount Strand", a line long since washed away but visible to his mind's eye. He wrote of boys continuing to play football after the light has faded and the lines of the pitch have become invisible:

Youngsters shouting their heads off in a field
As the light died and they kept on playing
Because by then they were playing in their heads …

Seamus Heaney's grace will play in our heads long after his earthly light has faded.

This obituary was first published in The Irish Times *on 31 August 2014.*

A journalist, columnist and drama critic, Fintan O'Toole is the Literary Editor of The Irish Times, *and the author of seven books, the most recent of which is* A History of Ireland in 100 Objects *(Royal Irish Academy, 2013).*

—

A COUNTERLIFE

—

Peter Sirr

In step with what escapes us.

A few years ago I was driving along a country road near Strokestown, Co Roscommon. It was dark and I was slightly nervous because I didn't know the road well and I was looking for the local secondary school in whose assembly hall Heaney would be giving a reading. Suddenly out of the darkness loomed a huge ash tree on whose branches I could make out a large cardboard sign with the words "Seamus Heaney" in luminous paint and an arrow pointing to a lane on the right.

The improvised sign, the reading that followed to a packed and enthralled audience, and the excitement afterwards, testified to a popularity and a rapport with readership and audience unusual even in a country that grants occasional notice to poets and poetry.

From the outset Heaney was a poet of extraordinary materiality: the visible world swarmed in to be reconstituted in dense stacks of language – those processions of thickly textured nouns and adjectives, that lust for exactitude, for a language that answered the demands of memory and clanged with the force of hammer on anvil.

What is it about this poetry that appeals to so many and that has, from the outset, earned itself critical acceptance and admiration of a kind rarely seen, establishing a consensus perhaps best summarized by Christopher Ricks when he called Heaney "the most trusted poet of our islands"?

Part of the appeal, certainly, lies in the subject matter. Heaney's consistent imaginative attention to his rural Co Derry upbringing affords many readers the sense, perhaps, that the life he expresses is part of a collective life of the spirit, the life of an Ireland that belongs to our sense of the past.

The verbal gifts that he brings to bear on his subjects give the work a sensual presence and an appeal to what he himself has called "the auditory imagination" that is hard to resist, in the way that Wordsworth, Hardy or Ted Hughes are hard to resist. There is the rich variety of the work: the poems of nature, the love poems, the poetry of memory, the translations, the essays. And yet, from the very beginning, a current of unease runs through the work, a sense that poetry, for all its aesthetic compensations, may not be enough, that the poet is poised, uncomfortably, between "politics and transcendence", between realism and celebration or between "the atrocious" and the counterlife of imaginative faith.

The narrative of Heaney's poetic career runs parallel to the political disintegration of Northern Ireland and the ensuing violence, and the uncertainty principle is closely linked to the poet's struggle to come to terms both with the violence itself and the poet's response to it. Heaney has had to bear the weight of public expectation – an expectation as ill defined as it was pervasive – that poetry should somehow answer to violence, division, rupture, that the poet speaks out of the public domain, that his voice must somehow be representative.

The poems are also concerned with art and its making, the articulation of his own search for a distinctive voice. The very first poem is "Digging", a self-conscious account of the vocation of art and a realization of how that calling will separate him from the world that the poems evoke:

Between my finger and my thumb
The squat pen rests.
I'll dig with it.

The lines seem canonical now, but "Digging" was a kind of initiation for Heaney; written in the summer of 1964 it was, he has said "the first poem I wrote where I thought my feelings had got into words ..."

Throughout his work memory is a trigger and a release into a sense of doubleness, of the intersection of the ordinary and the mysterious which comes through strongly in a poem such as "The Diviner", where, as in "The Forge" in *Door into the Dark*, an unnamed custodian of a profession that seems to border the real and the imaginary goes about his business until "The rod jerked with precise convulsions, / Spring water suddenly broadcasting / Through a green hazel its secret stations."

Heaney once said that in his earliest poems he tended to turn away from the immediate tensions – sectarianism, underlying violence – of Northern Ireland in favour of the impulse to write a more personal kind of poem, with Ted Hughes as a strong influence: "one part of my temperament took over: the private County Derry childhood part of myself rather than the slightly aggravated young Catholic male part." Yet one of the most striking poems in *Door into the Dark* – "Requiem for the Croppies" – is an explicit identification with his nationalist heritage. Written to commemorate the fiftieth anniversary of the Easter Rising, it returns instead to the 1798 Rebellion, and presents an image of continuity and resurrection through the voice of a dead "croppy": "The pockets of our greatcoats full of barley – / No kitchens on the run, no striking camp – / We moved quick and sudden in our own country."

Heaney's world is now so familiar to his readers that it's important to understand the degree to which his poems map experiences that were not readily available in Irish literature. He talked of how, for instance, the poetry of Louis MacNeice still felt distant to him, made him feel that he was still "up against the windowpane of literature." The world of poetry and literature seemed remote from "the world of state scholarships, the Gaelic Athletic Association, October devotions, the Clancy Brothers, buckets and egg-boxes where I had had my being."

This is why Patrick Kavanagh was such a vital figure – he gave Heaney permission to trust his own experience, to make poems, as had Kavanagh, out of "the unregarded data of the life I had lived", and "to dwell without cultural anxiety among the usual landmarks of your life."

The crucial collections of the 1970s, *Wintering Out*, *North* (1975) and *Field Work* (1979) see a deepening sense of the poet's vocation, accompanied by the opening out of the poems' perspectives with their forays into history and myth and also by a more charged sense of the poet's role and responsibilities. Landscape, language and history are intimately connected in these poems, and in them we can read the beginning of a certain kind of public poetry, as Heaney seeks ways to represent his own heritage imaginatively and to begin to cope with the fissures of a society now in deep conflict.

The later books all draw from the well of the past, and often revisit his own previous configurations of it, so that there is a constant dialogue with himself as poet. The poems in the later books are also sharpened by their awareness of mortality. Part of Heaney's backward glance is a consolidation of faith in the face of obliteration, as in the memorable image in "Clearances" of the felled chestnut tree which had been planted at his birth, "its heft and hush become a bright nowhere, / A soul ramifying and forever / Silent, beyond silence listened for."

Everyone will go back to their own poems for their own reasons; there is an astonishing richness of work to choose from. Again and again the poetry of Seamus Heaney discovered the release into pleasure that is one of the truest sources of all poetry, and if we attend to it we might learn, like the poet, to be in step with what escapes us. It is hard to believe he is no longer with us, but we can be certain of the enduring spirit and grace of the poetry.

This is an edited version of an introductory essay to Seamus Heaney: Collected Poems, *a 15-CD box set of Heaney reading 11 of his poetry collections, published by RTÉ. It was first published in* The Irish Times *on 31 August 2013.*

Peter Sirr is a poet, critic, editor and translator living in Dublin. His most collection of poems is The Thing Is *(The Gallery Press, 2009).*

———

MYSTIC OF THE ORDINARY
———

John Montague

Doing his work.

Recently I spoke in Enniskillen at the Happy Days Beckett festival, an event Seamus would have loved for its generosity of spirit. He, like myself, emerged from a riven Ulster, and the Methodist and Union Halls, Anglican cathedral, Roman Catholic church and even PSNI station of the town all turned into a vast theatre would have amused him greatly.

My talk was moderated by Seamus's son Michael (this newspaper's radio critic), who has inherited not just his father's laughing eyes of a striking dark brown unusual in Ireland but also his considerable charm. He was a lively and intelligent moderator, but afterwards he expressed concern to my wife, Elizabeth, about his father, who was in hospital, just for observation since he had bruised his head in a fall. But Seamus had been looking more and more fragile lately, almost a ghost of himself, and so both Elizabeth and I were concerned.

Still, in the way of these things, we were not prepared for the blow when it arrived, and I reproach myself for my reluctance to read the signs in his very rueful last volume, *Human Chain*, where, again and again, he returns to the wakehouse and the graveyard: "When the funeral bell tolls / The grass is all a-tremble."

In the fine sequence "Route 110" he evokes the atmosphere of rural almost-gaiety after a funeral:

The corpse house then a house of hospitalities
Right through the small hours, the ongoing card game
Interrupted constantly by rounds

Of cigarettes on plates, biscuits, cups of tea,
The antiphonal recital of known events
And others rare, clandestine, undertoned.

Later he writes with a kind of barely suppressed angry lyricism about, presumably, the victims of local violence:

... bodies
Unglorified, accounted for and bagged
Behind the grief cordons: not to be laid

In war graves with full honours, nor in a separate plot
Fired over on anniversaries
By units drilled and spruce and unreconciled.

Seamus's death comes, strangely enough, as we are still mourning the loss of the meticulous, industrious, eccentric and eminently generous Dennis O'Driscoll, whose series of interviews, published as *Stepping Stones*, are the best guide we have yet to the heart of Heaney. He was not Seamus's Boswell, however, but more of a confidant.

While Seamus seemed to be encased in courtesy like a medieval knight, he also relished what the Scots call flytings. Hugh MacDiarmid, for example, loved Norman MacCaig, but to hear their banter you would think they were enemies. To appreciate a bullseye scored against oneself was part of the game, and Seamus, for all his gravitas, had a frisky and wry sense of humour.

Once, walking in winter after an Irish Academy of Letters meeting, I remarked on his voluminous new overcoat, with a bright scarf at the throat, "Lord, Seamus! You're beginning to look like a bishop." He trumped me easily: "Why stop there?" he said with a grin.

When asked to pronounce on Seamus's death, a phrase coalesced in my mind: he did his work. That may sound like I was suggesting he wrote poems as if stoically or doggedly completing a job of work. But what I meant is that he realized his destiny. A gift and the fulfilment of its promise, the rounding out of a career, is a rare thing, but Seamus achieved it. And another phrase occurred to me, from Milton: "Nothing is here for tears, nothing to wail."

Destiny is to some degree bound up with geography, at least for poets of Northern rural background like Seamus and myself. I grew up in the rough hinterland of Tyrone, at the edge of the Clogher Valley. My literary imagination was influenced by the ghost of William Carleton, and I attended the junior seminary at Armagh in wartime, whereas Seamus lived along the Bann with its eel fisheries, and went to school at St Columb's, alongside Brian Friel, John Hume, Seamus Deane and Phil Coulter. (It has been suggested that they put something in the water at St Columb's, to produce such formidable Irishmen.) My part of Tyrone was smouldering, while Seamus's part of Derry was fairly placid, and this I suppose accounts for some of the differences in our verse, those nineteenth-century categories like "Fenian" or "AOH".

But when I first met Seamus, he gave me a book on the '98 Rebellion, which had inspired his "Requiem for the Croppies", whereas I was back with the O'Neills, and a family legend that one of my ancestors had offered hospitality to the soon-to-be-deposed James Stuart on his way to the Siege of Derry. From such frail conduits can poetry spring, but there was also the next football match.

Yet soon history would bear hard on us, from Bloody Sunday to the Omagh bombing, but before all that there was an all-too-brief period of bliss in Belfast, when Michael Emmerson's Belfast Festival was up and running. It was there I first heard the lyric triumvirate of Heaney, Derek Mahon and Michael Longley, later joined by Jimmy Simmons. Seán Ó Riada was named composer of the year, enchanting all with his double gift of classical and Irish music.

This was the rollicking background of the early Heaney, although his titles were sombre: *Death of a Naturalist* (1966) and *Door into the Dark* (1969). He and Marie, his wife, had found a fine house near Lavery's in Ashley Avenue, not far from the university at which he had begun to lecture. But before long the atmosphere in the North would darken. Seamus remains haunted, in his last book, by a terrible thing that happened on his own street, and he continues to wonder:

And what in the end was there left to bury
Of Mr Lavery, blown up in his own pub
As he bore the primed device and bears it still …

At the time, Seamus agonized over that incident in a poem, of which he sent me several revisions, with the crucial line "We petrify or uproot now."

And so they came south, where they created islands of graciousness in Dublin and Wicklow, and where Seamus refined and burnished his poetic gift. As I wrote of him in the *Dublin Literary Review*, "Like Hopkins, he is a mystic of the ordinary, which he renders extraordinary." The microscopic intensity of his gaze, coupled with the magnanimity of his vision, created poems of singular power. And people will miss the warm, friendly voice with which he read them.

Not long ago, after Iraq, after Afghanistan, Seamus remarked to me in a letter that the world had turned into "a big Ulster." So our own legacy of conflict and woe had spread across the globe. Yet one hopes the poet speaks to the conscience of peoples, speaks a truth that can heal, and redeem.

This obituary was first published in The Irish Times *on 7 September 2014.*

John Montague's latest volume of poetry is Speech Lessons *(Gallery Press, 2011). He lives in Co Cork.*

—

POSTSCRIPT
—

Dan Chiasson

The scale of things.

I learned that Seamus Heaney had died from a *New York Times* push notification, a feature on my phone that I keep intending to turn off. It was the saddest I have been about a poet's death since the death of James Merrill, in 1995, which I learned about, also upon waking, from the NPR broadcast that served as an alarm on my clock radio. Poets place their voices inside our heads, so close to our thoughts that it feels as though we've thought them up. It is odd when they make the news, which they do only occasionally, and only by making it very big, by winning the Nobel Prize, as Heaney did, and by dying. It is like learning from the media something secret about yourself, something you thought you'd kept well hidden.

Heaney's poems were full of finds, unlikely retrievals from the slime of the ground or the murk of history and memory. His poems about peat bogs and what they preserve are probably the most important English-language poems written in the past 50 years about violence–the "intimate, tribal revenge" that underscores the news. But they never stray an inch from the personal tone that Heaney honed in his poems about his four-year-old brother's death or his mother's method of slicing potatoes into soup. That the same vocabulary, the same notes and the same intelligence could govern his personal poems and his political ones only pointed to the arbitrariness of the distinction.

Just as a peat bog might contain an elk skeleton, a stick of butter, or the entire, snug corpse of a murder victim, the "word hoard" of English held, for Heaney, infinite discoveries. When he was commissioned to translate *Beowulf*, he said he found the task onerous until he had a breakthrough: he discovered in the Anglo-Saxon text a word he remembered his grandmother using that he hadn't heard since – "thole", which means "suffer." Everything about this epiphany is classic Heaney: finding the seed of English poetry, *Beowulf*, on the tip of his grandmother's tongue; finding a word so downcast in a memory so warm, the mingled pain and sweetness, history and the hearth.

We all carry around our favorite Heaney. Mine is "Squarings", his brilliant sequence of not-quite-sonnets, named after a term from marbles. In these poems, the rectangular shape of the sonnet is "squared" by lopping off the couplet. The resulting twelve lines, four neat tercets, draw upon the oblique angles of childhood, the only time in our life when we know what being very small is like, and the time when we are most likely to be flush with the earth, on our knees or bellies or sides in the dirt:

I was four but I turned four hundred maybe
Encountering the ancient dampish feel
Of a clay floor. Maybe four thousand even.

Anyhow, there it was. Milk poured for cats
In a rank puddle-place, splash-darkened mould
Around the terra cotta water-crock

Ground of being. Body's deep obedience
To all its shifting tenses. A half-door
Opening directly into starlight.

Out of that earth house I inherited
A stack of singular, cold memory-weights
To load me, hand and foot, in the scale of things.

The work of these poems is to make as real as possible the represented sensory experiences of the child, conveying their aromas and textures as though at first hand. Perhaps no poet has ever been better at this one thing. For Heaney, being a writer means going wherever it takes to find "the scale of things", even doing what he describes the young Thomas Hardy doing in a later poem in the sequence:

Once, as a child, out in a field of sheep,
Thomas Hardy pretended to be dead
And lay down flat among their dainty shins.

In that sniffed-at, bleated-into, grassy space
He experimented with infinity.
His small cool brow was like an anvil waiting

For sky to make it sing the perfect pitch
Of his dumb being, and that stir he caused
In the fleece-hustle was the original

Of a ripple that would travel eighty years
Outward from there, to be the same ripple
Inside him at its last circumference.

The minute and crabbed always opens out into "infinity", whose dimensions are only glimpsed from the confines of a room, the arbitrary boundaries of a game of marbles or a short poem in regular stanzas.

Heaney's poems made you feel confided in, addressed at close range; he was like that in person, too. A couple of memories: Twenty-two years ago, my roommates and I crawled out of the muck and slime of our dorm rooms to hear Heaney read to a packed house in Johnson Chapel, at Amherst College. When I picture that room, I always think of Robert Frost's description of a cup filled "to the brim / And even above the brim." Students were splayed everywhere, in the aisles and on the backs of pews. Later, at a party at a professor's house, we ate myriad shrimps and tried to look at home drinking wine. Heaney spent an inordinate amount of time laughing and joking with us, until his attention turned sharply to the door: Joseph Brodsky had arrived, so disheveled his clothes appeared to be on sideways. A few years later, at a department Christmas party at Harvard, Heaney infiltrated the large bloc of graduate students looking postmodern by the Xeroxes and made mischievous jokes about colleagues. When his wine glass was empty, as it always seemed to be, he told us, "Wait right here; don't go anywhere." He made a beeline to where the wine bottles were, filled his cup, and came right back, just the way he'd promised.

This obituary first appeared online as a blog.

A poet, critic and journalist, Dan Chiasson is the author of six books of poetry and criticism. His latest collection of poems is Bicentennial *(Knopf, 2014).*

——

THE COMEDY OF SEAMUS HEANEY

——

Robert Pinsky

Perfect timing.

Irreverent comedy subverts, but it doesn't necessarily hurt. Its best laughter can be derisive, but not cruel.

Seamus Heaney, among many other things, embodied that central principle: his comic sense was gleefully sharp, but it was not mean. I think he disdained cruelty, as well as pomposity. Mischievous, more bite than bark in the sense that it was mordant with minimal rhetoric, Heaney was not genteel. He enjoyed the disrespectful roar of impropriety.

Examples? Here's a story he told me, about an Irish literary eminence who was invited to a dinner party attended by the young William Butler Yeats. In those days the youthful emerging poet Yeats was at his most affected: a cape-wearing aesthete, with a lock of hair falling over his pale brow, and a distracted, ethereal manner.

The eminence was asked, the next morning, "Well, you've met the young Yeats – what did you think of him?"

Seamus, already chortling, delivered the answer at Full Twinkle, and possibly amping the Irish accent a bit:

"Think of him? *Think* of him, is it? I think he should be put back in and fooked-for again!"

To be put back in and fucked-for again – surreal, and wonderfully clear. As I remember, he repeated the phrase, relishing it two or three times. But maybe the important element in the story, and Seamus's pleasure in it, is the implicit rejection of piety about the great poet ... maybe, as a further implication, about *any* great poet. From that perspective, the story is satirical not about Yeats so much as it is about Yeats-olatry.

Another memory takes the irreverence further and wider. It may not seem funny in writing (a prosy example of You Had To Be There). One evening, over drinks for five or six people in a living room, someone got the idea of portraying the deaths of great poets as represented by fingers. So, for John Keats the finger vibrates a bit with a series of coughs, then goes flat. For Hart Crane, the right finger rides the rising and falling ship of the left hand for a time, then jumps off, then after a moment it sinks out of view.

Seamus knew which Irish poet had been executed by firing squad, and his fingers portrayed that awful event. Someone did Shelley drowning in the storm. Poe and Dylan Thomas both wheeled and reeled until the index finger representing each of them collapsed. Someone did Lorca. Someone else mimed how Marlowe, portrayed as a right-hand finger, was stabbed, after a struggle, by his left-hand opponent. Yes, I confess that Plath putting her head into the oven, too, was portrayed. The variety of the deaths, and how many of them that group of inebriated people could remember. Berryman waved from his bridge.

I hope that our silly game was a form of tribute.

Other nights, it was the straight-ahead, classic joke, with the buildup and punch line: a folk-form that in my experience is mastered mainly by Jews, American Southerners, and the Irish. The test is not merely skill in the telling but the size of the teller's repertoire. A real joke teller can reach for hundreds, and disperse them over sociable hours, arranging them by associative categories and topics: the doctor's office, the farm, the hotel, and of course the bar.

He enjoyed the disrespectful roar of impropriety.

I will not recount a joke here: the form, like lyric poetry – more so – is essentially vocal. And the kind of joke expertise I mean, as well as vocal, is also social. Beyond the texture of timing within the fabric of each joke there is structural timing: a social sense that governs the overall constellation, the movement from teller to teller and from joke to the next joke. (The next "story" as the novelist William Kennedy, another maestro, would say.) You need a sense of when to tell which joke when, in which version, in which company.

In other words, the good joke teller has a sense of occasion. And I have never known anyone with a finer sense of occasion than Seamus Heaney.

Not that he was a perfect joke teller. Dialect, for instance, was not his *métier*, so like a true devotee of the form he exploited his incompetence for laughs. A particular joke I like, set in hell, requires an Italian accent and a German one for two essential characters. When Seamus tried to tell the joke, both characters sounded kind of Japanese, as someone pointed out, much to Seamus's amusement. Among his blessed traits was an ability to laugh, with wholehearted pleasure, at himself.

This obituary was first published online on The Daily Beast.

One of America's most celebrated poets, Robert Pinsky was the Poet Laureate of the Unites States from 1997 to 2000. He is the author of 15 books of poetry and criticism, most recently Selected Poems *(Farrar, Straus and Giroux, 2011).*

———

ON THE FAR SIDE OF REVENGE: THE PLAYS OF SEAMUS HEANEY

———

Srila Nayak

No flinching at fate.

By 2003, Sophocles' *Antigone*, a fifth-century BC tragedy about a violent confrontation between a defiant young woman and an arrogant ruler, was one of the most widely adapted plays in Ireland.

When Seamus Heaney was invited to translate *Antigone* for the Abbey Theatre's centenary program in early 2003, he wondered, "How many *Antigones* could Irish theater put up with?" The multiple retellings had employed the Greek tragedy as a form of reckoning with contemporary geopolitical crises — wars, injustices, moral and political corruption, and dictatorships.

Conall Morrison's much-lauded adaptation set the play in the context of a suicide bombing and global terrorism in the early 2000s. Tom Paulin and Brendan Kennelly's versions transported the play to a troubled Northern Ireland in the last third of the twentieth century. When Heaney undertook his own version of the play, renaming it *The Burial at Thebes* (2004), he had arrived at a solution to the dangers of staleness and repetition – a mingling of poetry and politics.

Seamus Heaney, who recently died at the age of 74, once confessed that drama offered him greater artistic freedom than poetry. In his plays – adaptations and translations of Sophocles' Greek tragedies – the dramatic action involves the nitty-gritty of ethical dilemmas and human life, balancing impassioned rhetoric with transparent sentiment.

While Heaney authored over a dozen collections of poetry, he wrote only two plays – both in verse – *The Cure at Troy* (1990) and *The Burial at Thebes*. The plays offer an interesting study of contrasts: they are balanced between the archaic and modern, between invention and adaptation, between politics and aesthetics. Both plays were commissioned by theaters in Ireland and they remain very much enmeshed in questions of the nature of literary forms and fractious contemporary politics in Ireland and elsewhere, and how best to bring together politics and dramatic form.

His first play, *The Cure at Troy*, a version of Sophocles' *Philoctetes*, dramatizes the deep rift between individual morality and patriotic duty. Oedipus and Neoptolemus, the young son of the dead warrior Achilles, plot ways to either lure Philoctetes to Troy, or somehow procure Hercules's bow and arrows, which are in Philoctetes' possession. According to a prophecy, Hercules' weapons would help the Greeks win the war against the Trojans.

Philoctetes is the Sophoclean version of Caliban, an outcast from society suffering from the curse of an incurable, foul-smelling wound, living a brutish life on the desolate island of Lemnos. He was "marooned", left to perish on Lemnos by Odysseus and other Greek soldiers after they could no longer withstand his howls of pain and the stench of his wound.

Neoptolemus is charged by Odysseus to obtain the bow and arrows from Philoctetes by stealth and cunning, and the chief tension of the play turns on the conflict between Neoptolemus's natural desire to not wrong Philoctetes and his obligations to his fellow Greek warriors.

After ten years in the wilderness of exile, Philoctetes is more animal than human; he continues to suffer terribly from his wound and is consumed by his rage toward Odysseus and his former Greek compatriots. In Heaney's brilliantly balanced rendition, Philoctetes is a victim of the wily Odysseus, but he is also his own worst foe; the Chorus admonishes him,

"Your wound is what you feed on, Philoctetes." But Philoctetes is also a Greek hero, who ultimately regains his lost glory when Neoptolemus persuades him to rejoin the Greeks and fight the Trojans: "The hero that was healed and then went on to heal the wound of the Trojan war itself."

Heaney would have found in the notion of a healing of a suppurating wound the echoes of the possibility of the reconstruction "of the wounded spots on the face of the earth" – "of Ulster and Israel and Bosnia and Rwanda." In an interview, Heaney explains that his decision to rename *Philoctetes* and call it the *The Cure at Troy* was inspired by Irish Catholic religious beliefs. "In Ireland, north and south, the idea of a miraculous cure is deeply lodged in the religious subculture …"

Neoptolemus's struggle between his duty toward the Greeks and his innate moral principles held a special allure for Heaney. His spiritual battle became a metaphor for the dilemma faced by Catholics and Protestants in Northern Ireland – would, to paraphrase Heaney, speaking truthfully on certain occasions mean that you are letting down your side? The hidden connection between Sophoclean theater and Irish politics emerges vividly in Heaney's 1995 Nobel lecture in a searing criticism of the notion of a too-narrowly conceived "political solidarity" that blinded one to "poetic truth" and the change that could transpire when Catholics and Protestants could reach beyond sectarian loyalties and partisanship to forge fragile alliances.

In Neoptolemus's decision to rise above the "side" of his peers and generously bring Philoctetes back to human society, to the sphere of fellowship, influence and power, Heaney glimpsed an ideal order, an alternative to the long history in Northern Ireland of "hardening attitudes and narrowing possibilities … of political solidarity, traumatic suffering and sheer emotional self-protectiveness."

Heaney took some liberties with his translation of *Philoctetes*, a notable change being the addition of an extra chorus to the play, which, ironically, went on to become the most famous lines in *The Cure at Troy* (Nadine Gordimer called her 1999 book of essays *Living in Hope and History*):

But then, once in a lifetime
The longed for tidal wave
Of justice can rise up,
And hope and history rhyme.

For a poet of elegies on lairs of ossified bones and skeletons in peat bogs and marshes, who called himself "Hamlet the Dane", "skull handler" and "smeller of rot", this choric verse is undeniably optimistic and hopeful about the value of human action. However, after watching performances of *The Cure at Troy*, Heaney questioned the value of the intersection between contemporary politics and dramatic aesthetics. He wondered if the play's anachronistic, modern choric references to the "innocent in gaols", "hunger strikes" and "the police widow" couldn't be faulted for a certain intrusive didacticism: "Once the performances started, I came to realize the topical references were a mistake. Spelling things out like that is almost like patronizing the audience."

Heaney's ambitions for his later play, *The Burial at Thebes*, are decidedly artistic in nature – a desire for greater fidelity to the original *Antigone* and a quest for the right sort of poetic meter. Heaney's version of *Antigone* was commissioned for the Abbey's centenary program in the midst of America's global war on terror, the invasion of Iraq and the erosion of civil liberties. The political circumstances were certainly ripe for a play on the unchecked powers of a ruler and the arbitrarily imposed distinctions between a traitor and a patriot. Heaney's adaptation of Sophocles' drama was also meant to complete an Irish literary tradition that had started when W.B. Yeats had adapted Sophocles' *Oedipus at Colonus* and *Oedipus the King* for the Abbey in the 1930s.

At the heart of the play is the issue of the burial of Antigone's brother Polyneices. Labeling him a traitor, Creon orders his corpse to be left unburied, to decompose in the open air and to be devoured by animals and birds. Antigone defies Creon's tyrannical edict and performs burial rituals for Polyneices. Flinging aside Creon's mortal law, Antigone's claims to act under the greater charge of an immutable god-given moral compass, "Religion dictates the burial of the dead." Heaney renamed his version of the play *The Burial at Thebes*, placing front and center not the titular heroine of Sophocles' play, but also the object of savage persecution and violence – the corpse of a presumed traitor.

Heaney's adaptation wrestles with the question of how to make an "overfamiliar" play pulsate with captivating voices and poetic rhythms of such metrical variety that the modern viewer would find the play a profound and joyful experience. Heaney, who was not familiar with Greek and worked from multiple translations of each play (some of which closely followed the "metrical shifts of the original Greek"), called his endeavor "an ongoing line-by-line, hand-to-hand engagement with the material."

In order to capture the right meter and pitch for the modern stage, Heaney turned to an eighteenth-century Irish lament in the voice of a woman who is grieving over the body of her husband lying on a roadside in County Cork in much the same way as Antigone is distraught that Polyneices' corpse is abandoned outside Thebes. The poem furnished Heaney with the lean, deft and conversational meter ("the three-beat line") to fashion dialogue as well as the voice, tone and pitch of the play for contemporary audiences; Heaney also employed a mix of the Old English Anglo-Saxon meter from Christian hymns and the traditional iambic pentameter.

Here is the crystalline, sharp and quietly wrenching speech of Antigone after she is condemned to die by Creon:

> No flinching then at fate.
> No wedding guests. No wake.
> No keen. No panegyric.
> I close my eye on the sun.
> I turn my back on the light.

The singular achievement of Heaney's verse drama is that it fulfills his own fond hopes for an art that is "not only pleasurably right but compellingly wise, not only a surprising variation played upon the world, but a retuning of the world itself."

This obituary first appeared online as a blog.

Srila Nayak works for the online journal Howlround. *She has a PhD in English Literary and Cultural Studies from Carnegie Mellon University and an MS in Journalism from Columbia University.*

———

TRIBUTE: AT THE AMERICAN ACADEMY

Karl Kirchwey

Back in Rome.

Seamus Heaney, who died in Dublin on Friday at the age of 74, was the William B. Hart Poet in Residence at the American Academy in Rome for three weeks in May of this year. In addition to being a major poet writing in English, he was a loyal friend to many other poets, including this one. Seamus was blessed, not only with a huge poetic gift, but also with a deep humanity and maturity. The seriousness with which he took his craft (in his own evolution, he spoke of "earning the right to be a poet") meant that the backbiting and power games that characterize some of the impoverished cantons of contemporary poetry were completely alien to him. His sights were set elsewhere, his masters were Virgil and Dante, and his hooded dark gaze and his sumptuous brogue always shamed you out of any petty grievance you might have. His courage could be felt, both in national terms – his refusal to be co-opted, as a poet, by the politics of his tormented country – and in personal ones, as he made his way back, slowly and with the determined help of his wife Marie and his family, from a major stroke some years ago. His poem "Miracle" refracts his own experience through the Gospel story of the healing of the paralytic, and it is completely characteristic of Seamus's human depth that the focus is not on the patient, but on those who help him:

> Not the one who takes up his bed and walks
> But the ones who have known him all along
> And carry him in …

I knew Seamus first in my capacity as Director of the Poetry Center of the 92nd Street Y in New York, where he read from his work throughout his career. One of my most vivid memories is of the staged reading of Seamus's translation of Sophocles' *Philoctetes* (called *The Cure At Troy*) that we presented in the Y's Kaufmann Concert Hall on St Patrick's Day in 1993. Seamus's friend, the poet and playwright Derek Walcott, was directing, and a cast of actors was assembled from as far away as California and Ireland. A major spring blizzard engulfed the north-eastern United States just in time to knock all plans for the play awry, but in spite of this the show went on, with Irish pipes and drums, with Roscoe Lee Browne, as the wounded Greek archer and hero, howling with pain and shambling about the stage in an old raincoat, and with a dinner reception afterwards at an Irish steakhouse where the Bushmills flowed freely. Throughout the vicissitudes of the theater, Seamus never lost his sense of humor. And the lines of his play, which so brilliantly redirects Sophocles' myth of injustice, grudge-bearing and forgiveness into the context of contemporary Ireland, are still echoing, I think, in that oak-panelled hall:

> Human beings suffer,
> They torture one another,
> They get hurt and they get hard.
> No poem or play or song
> Can fully right a wrong
> Inflicted and endured.

Seamus read those lines in the courtyard of the McKim, Mead and White building in May, during an event that had been threatened by rain but was a triumph, the culmination of his visit to the AAR. Weeks before his arrival in Rome, the demands for his time and his attention began to come in, and he navigated all of them with patience and grace, obliging as many people as he could. I listened to Seamus read his work several times, during those weeks in Rome – at the Casa delle Letterature, at the home of the Irish Ambassador to Italy, and finally at the AAR – and each time was reminded of how crucial his poems have been to my own understanding of what poetry can do and how life can be felt and understood. I listened as Seamus was interviewed more than once. Like any experienced public figure, he had certain conversational touchstones, certain repeating mottoes; but in his case, they seem unforgettable rather than ephemeral. "The work of art is finished and steady, a response and a resistance to desolation," he said. He quoted his great predecessor W.B. Yeats to the effect that "I have tried to hold in a single thought reality and justice." He remarked that "Language in Ireland is solidified history." And when asked whether or not he feared death, he responded, "I think literature has helped. Mythology has helped." Seamus provided no easy answers about what role poetry could possibly have, in a violent world. On the one hand, he quoted the question posed by the poet Czesław Miłosz, who lived through the Nazi occupation of Poland: "What is poetry that does not save nations or people?" And Miłosz's answer to this was "The song of drunkards." For Miłosz, confronted with the atrocities of the twentieth century, poetry had to have a political dimension. On the other hand, Seamus also quoted his friend Joseph Brodsky, exiled as a "social parasite" from the Soviet Union, who declared that "If art teaches us anything, it is that the human condition is private." What Brodsky meant was that, given a totalitarian state, the most important thing about poetry is not its public voice, but its ability to articulate the individual consciousness. For Seamus, I think this difficult balance between public and private was crucial to poetry; and in his own work, it is what makes him a great poet.

During that reading in the McKim, Mead and White courtyard, Seamus presented a generous retrospective of his work, and in fact the poems artfully traced the evolution of consciousness and writing itself, from childhood through maturity, in sacred, secular and mythic terms. The jasmine was in flower on the walls of the building, and sparrows were noisy inside that jasmine. Arriving at a line in one of his poems that mentions birdsong, Seamus just held up his arm for a moment in silence. Nature itself, you see, was in concert with this poet. I will always cherish that image of Seamus, as I will always feel the last lines of the last poem he read, entitled "Postscript" and describing a car trip in the west of Ireland, which responds both to Yeats's "The Wild Swans at Coole" and to the violence of Yeats's other swan poem, about Leda:

> You are neither here nor there,
> A hurry through which known and strange things pass
> As big soft buffetings come at the car sideways
> And catch the heart off guard and blow it open.

Seamus Heaney caught our hearts off guard; he blew them open. That is what poetry can do.

This obituary first appeared on the website of the American Academy in Rome.

Karl Kirchwey is the Director of Program in Creative Writing at Boston University. His seventh book of poems, Stumbling Blocks: Roman Poems, *is forthcoming.*

—

CLEAN NEW MUSIC: ON SEAMUS HEANEY

—

Trent Morris

Trust in rightness.

1

I don't think I ever quite knew myself until I read Seamus Heaney. I can't remember exactly which of his poems I read first, but that's not important. What is important is what his poems did to me. When I encountered "Blackberry Picking", I first felt the full force of what a poem can do. The poem describes picking blackberries in the spring and hoarding them in a tub in the barn, then discovering that they have begun to rot, ending with the lines "It wasn't fair / That all the lovely canfuls smelt of rot. / Each year I'd hoped they'd keep, knew they would not." The poem hit me somewhere right at the base of my ribs. It created an actual physical sensation. When I was a kid, I was always catching small animals, usually crickets and frogs, and keeping them in coffee cans, then forgetting about them for days, only to return and find their corpses. I remember the mingled smell of dead crickets and Folgers coffee – those once-lovely canfuls.

For a long time, that same feeling, that of my own emotions synching up with those described by a poem, eluded description. For me, it was ineffable. The connection with a poem, with a poet, while one of the strongest that I felt, sidestepped definition. Appropriately though, in his essay "Feelings Into Words", collected in *Preoccupations*, Heaney provided an answer for the question he had raised:

> Finding a voice means that you can get your own feeling into your
> own words and that your words have the feel of you about them;
> and I believe that it may not even be a metaphor, for a poetic voice
> is probably very intimately connected with the poet's natural
> voice, the voice that he hears as the ideal speaker of the lines he is
> making up. How, then, do you find it? In practice, you hear it
> coming from somebody else; you hear something in another

writer's sounds that flows in through your ear and enters the echo chamber of your head and delights your whole nervous system in such a way that your reaction will be, "Ah, I wish I had said that, in that particular way." This other writer, in fact, has spoken something essential to you, something you recognize instinctively as a true sounding of aspect of yourself and your experience.

For me, Heaney was the place where I definitively heard that voice in several aspects – from his content down to individual phrases and chunks of sound. Heaney wrote, especially in his early volumes, of life in rural Northern Ireland and all that entailed, from the loss of a livelihood earned through manual labor and agriculture in *Death of a Naturalist* and *Door Into the Dark* to the way in which the political concerns of the Troubles were embedded in the very archaeology of the place in his *magnum opus*, *North*. The sense of place in his poetry is extraordinary. For me, his content choices were much more than examples of Heaney taking up the old poetic mortar and pestle of "to be universal, you must be local"; they unfolded the world of poetry for me in places where I didn't even realize there were creases.

2

My father grew up on a rabbit farm and helped his father poach from the National Forest for supper, while my mother's family of nine planted five acres of potatoes to live on through the winter, her father making his meager living skidding pine logs with mules. My mother's family didn't have indoor plumbing until the late 1960s and used a dug well, complete with bucket and windlass, for water. Home for me is the Ouachita Mountains, a place even more innocuous then pre-Troubles Ulster: a small mountain range 500 miles from the ass end of the Appalachians.

In Heaney's voice I found a license, almost an imperative, to write about the basic things that I had grown up around; if Heaney's Moyola and Castledawson and Mossbawn mattered and had something profound to offer the world, so did my own region straddling the Arkansas–Oklahoma state line. I should have seen this before; I had been reading Frost and certainly could have picked up the same things from him, but, lovely as Frost is, his New England didn't resonate with me in the same contorted but insistent ways that Heaney's Northern Ireland did. Why is that? For me, it amounts to how I identified with Heaney's voice.

Heaney's voice went much deeper than regionalism, not only in his persistent archaeological motifs, which critics have identified as representative of the collective unconscious, but also in the basic noise of his poems – the tangible aural sensations that create meaning almost independent from the semantics of the language, scraping down even further into the unconscious. When Heaney writes of bringing his grandfather "milk in a bottle corked sloppily with paper", he works nearly with onomatopoeia, what his mentor Philip Hobsbaum termed "Heaneyspeak", which I find to be little more than a cute way of referring to Heaney's poetic voice. Heaney's obsession with sound (again, something I might have, in another life, first noticed in Frost and his "sound of sense") struck me immediately. In "Blackberry Picking", the line "where briars scratched and wet grass bleached our boots" provided a perfect nugget of voice, marrying sound – the words "briars scratched" and "bleached our boots" make the exact sound as the actions that they describe – with the larger concern of identifiable content. I have bleached a couple pairs of boots myself.

3

I find a rightness, for lack of a better term, in Heaney's voice on all levels. I don't need to try to find exactly how the position of the tongue in pronouncing "Poised like mud grenades, their blunt heads farting" perfectly encapsulates the lines' meaning, nor do I have to search for the tenuous relationship between Heaney's description of the fearful transformation from tadpole to bullfrog in "Death of a Naturalist" with my own experience of catching and hatching tadpoles and being frightened by the plop of bullfrogs in my grandmother's pond. Heaney's voice is true, and it is readily apparent. That is enough. I don't need the critics or Carl Jung to tell me that depictions of amphibian fear tap into the collective unconscious and that the water of the flax dam represents sex, further reinforced by the reproduction of the frogs, etc. I read the poem and I know, in a very visceral way, that Heaney has gotten something very right, that his voice has executed a perfect arpeggio in a brilliant cadenza.

4

"Blackberry Picking" offered up yet another lesson in voice years after I first read it. I had always heard the poem in my own accent, and read it with my own voice. In a dialect that is firmly within the sphere of the upper American South, the only apparent rhyme in the poem is "clot/knot." I had once read an essay that alluded to the "effective use of slant rhyme in the poem", but did not offer any examples. I quickly assumed that the reference to "slant rhyme" was a mistake. Coming from a dialect which monophthongizes long "i" sounds to a fronted "ah" and merges the pronunciation of "pin" and "pen" to both sound as "pin", the words "sun" and "ripen" don't even come close to rhyming. The stress patterns of my own speech didn't help. The word "ripen" is always pronounced with the stress on the first syllable, the second is diminished to the point of barely even being voiced. This manner of speech, which formed and forms my own internal reading voice, tends to take iambic pentameter out back for a good woodshedding, never mind that I didn't really learn to even recognize iambs for a long while after encountering Heaney. In short, while the poem managed to strike me with great force, I was missing what amounts to half of Heaney's craftsmanship. I didn't discover any of this until I actually heard recordings of Heaney reading the poem, the way he heard it, in his own natural voice. Not only was every line in iambic pentameter, but every line rhymed in an array of brilliant little half rhymes. The heavens opened and light shone down, illuminating, if nothing else, the full extent of Heaney's skill.

5

In Heaney's fifth volume, *North*, he creates and interprets Ireland through its long history of Germanic incursions beginning with the Vikings. In the title poem, he imagines the voices of dead Vikings as "ocean-deafened voices" and "the longship's swimming tongue", which tells him:

> ... "Lie down
> in the word-hoard, burrow
> the coil and gleam
> of your furrowed brain.
>
> Compose in darkness.
> Expect aurora borealis
> in the long foray
> but no cascade of light.

Keep your eye clear
as the bleb of the icicle,
trust the feel of what nubbed treasure
your hands have known."

In appropriating this archaeological voice, Heaney delivers a series of admonishments that are instructions to the poet as well as the reader. This voice is different, more ancient – unmetered stresses, no rhymes. It's no wonder that Heaney wound up translating *Beowulf*; he was familiar with its voice, able to call it up from the "belly of stone ships", to utter its implorement: "trust the feel of what nubbed treasure / your hands have known." This imperative struck me. "Trust!" it said; whatever your hands have known, trust in it. As long as your eye is clear, trust. Lie down. Burrow. Like Antaeus, be nourished by the soil, by a sense of place. Trust your place, trust your own geography, trust in your own culture, trust your own experience.

For Heaney, this experience, this nubbed treasure, like all good treasures, is buried. As a poet, Heaney exhumes things. In "Bogland", the last poem from *Door into the Dark*, he writes of the bringing up of ancient artifacts from Irish bogs, and that the bogs themselves "might be Atlantic seepage. / The wet centre is bottomless." Speaking about the poem in an essay, Heaney notes that he derived the last line from hearing old people tell children not to play in the bogs because they were bottomless. This mining of memory is essential to Heaney's poetry. In trying to access things that Heaney only half-consciously knows, he bores into my unconscious as a reader – the things that I too am only half-aware of. Maybe that's why the feeling I get reading Heaney approaches inexplicable, conveyed only through metaphors of physical sensation: what Heaney has to say does something to my subconscious; his voice resonates there on that low level. It takes up residence with all the archetypes and shadows in the part of my psyche that, if mapped, would be labeled "Here Be Monsters" in ornate script wreathed in a facsimile of fog.

6

Heaney's most famous poem, "Digging", set the tenor for his early work, celebrating the subterranean and particularly the role that writing plays in exploring it. The poem describes the memories Heaney has of his father and grandfather digging, but laments that "I've no spade to follow men like them", then goes on to assert, "Between my finger and my thumb / the squat pen rests. / I'll dig with it." Like his grandfather, who digs up turf for fuel, Heaney unearths a fuel that is no less important. Heaney once remarked that, to someone from his background, the word "work" meant physical work only, that one could not be "upstairs reading a book and say 'oh, I'm working'", and that "Digging" was partly a defense of his own way of life against the mores of his own culture. "Digging" shows the conflict between tradition and modernity. In this way it participates, in a meaningful way, in the development of Western thought. To be egregiously brief, the Ancient, Medieval, and Modern periods can be said to be concerned with humanity's perception of conflict with three different iterations of higher power. The ancients conceived of gods who dealt out inescapable fate, then gods were replaced with a singular God who, though he was all powerful, still managed to allow evil in the world. Most recently, God has been replaced with science and technology. Their conflict with humanity was probably first noticed by the Romantics and has persisted, more or less, until the present day. Heaney knew and lived that conflict – of watching his father's occupation of cattle dealer fade away. It is equally important to me, in very practical terms. My grandfather worked in the timber, cutting down trees for a living; the next generation, my mother's two brothers, were both carpenters, building houses from those same trees. My grandfather had a fourth-grade education; my uncles finished only high school; I became a college boy and sure as hell can't start cutting down trees for a living. In both a metaphorical and literal sense, all the trees have already been cut.

Maybe "Digging" seems old hat. It was written in the mid-1960s and was one of Heaney's first poems. However, there is a reason that it is Heaney's most anthologized poem. Its strident voice proclaims that poetry, that literature, is important in a time when the nutritional label on a box of Post-Toasties is considered a text and given equal status with Keats's odes.

7

In "The Forge", Heaney plainly states in the first line, "All I know is a door into the dark", then goes on to describe a blacksmith who "expends himself in shape and music", who, upon looking out his door at the passing lights of traffic, turns back inside "To beat real iron out, to work the bellows." For a long time I read Heaney as looking out into the dark from inside the blacksmith shop, but I was wrong. Blacksmith shops are always dark so that the smith can properly see the color of the metal he's working; different temperatures are indicated by the color, from reds to yellows and whites, each ideal for specific tasks: cutting, welding, drawing. Heaney looks in on this dark smithy; he has the capacity to see it, his eye is "clear as the bleb of the icicle." His vantage point standing, as it were, with one foot in the past and another in the present allows him to see this murky scene. All his foundational knowledge is in these old ways; his family did not own a car when he was growing up, and his father plowed their fields with horses. Heaney "beats real iron out" as he dredges up these artifacts. The farther down one goes into the ground, the older things are, back even to the Iron Age: this is the basic tenet of geology and archaeology. Heaney is connected to these old, chthonic things. He disinters them and remembers them. In a sense, he members them again, creates them anew through his writing.

8

Heaney gives the best explanation of what he does in the last poem of *Death of a Naturalist*. "Personal Helicon" is a poem about wells and Heaney's fascination with them. Various wells are characterized as "So deep you saw no reflection in it", "fructified" with "long roots" and in particular one that "had echoes, gave back your own call / with a clean new music in it." He ends the poem with:

> Now, to pry into roots, to finger slime,
> To stare, big-eyed Narcissus, into some spring
> Is beneath all adult dignity. I rhyme
> To see myself, to set the darkness echoing.

Heaney claims to see himself, not necessarily as an unadulterated reflection, but through echoes that come back up from the wells that he has dug into the darkness. The darkness of this well, bored into the deep strata of the unconscious, echoes with his voice and gives back a "clean new music." Heaney writes as a means to hear himself, in order to truly ascertain his own voice. To do this he must work in the underground medium of his upbringing. It is the darkness that must be used to create the echo. The well must be dug deep, into those long, fructified roots of the subconscious, before it can echo. The discovery of this well and its echo is an exhumation, and even a bit of a resurrection. Though they are echoes, that "clean new music" carries a ring that comes from beyond the grave. And what grave is as deep as a well?

9

In hearing Heaney's voice echoing, I was able to get a sense of my own voice. I could use, at first at least, Heaney's well to shout in, to see what came back, to find what those fructified roots are made of. Eventually I need to dig my own well, into my own fructified roots, with its own echo. Of course my own well may tap into the same underground spring as Heaney's — perhaps all wells do — but I first needed Heaney's well to become aware of what a well can do — of what digging can do. I needed Heaney's voice to know what a voice could sound like, and through Heaney I discovered my own voice. I learned to listen to the timbre of its echoes.

10

Seamus Heaney recently passed away. It was reported that his last words were a text message to his wife that read "*Noli timere*", which, translated into good King James English, is "Be not afraid." Of course, Seamus was sharp enough to alter the conjugation from *nolite timere*, found in St Matthew, which is in the second-person plural to the singular *noli*. This surprised me, not because a dying man still knew enough Latin to not only quote from the Vulgate but to give the proper conjugation on the fly, but rather than Heaney's last words were via text message. My perception of him as a poet of the soil, one who spoke of thatched roofs and plowing by hand, was shattered by the news of his last words being transmitted via text message. Of course I read this news on a smartphone, but somehow it was still a staggering blow.

It only took me five minutes of careful thought to reestablish equilibrium. So what if Heaney and cellphones seemed incongruous to me? His life as a man of letters probably seemed just as contradictory to the people of his childhood. From the external world to our senses, from our senses to our brains, from our brains into language, from that language into writing, from the handwritten original to print in a book, from a printed book through the whole shebang again, back through taps of thumbs into a text message and radio waves, beams of invisible light, and a torrent of ones and zeros – it's all just space between the infinite notches of Plato's divided line.

Philo Farnsworth, inventor of the first electronic image pickup device that made television possible, was inspired by furrows of plowed earth and envisioned a device which reproduced images by scanning then reproducing them one row at a time. It wasn't nearly as incongruous as I had thought. Heaney writes in his "Glanmore Sonnets" that

Now the good life could be to cross a field
And art a paradigm of earth new from the lathe
Of ploughs. My lea is deeply tilled.

Arting a paradigm, that's our real business. The medium doesn't matter. Give us dancing electrons. Be not afraid. Dig with them.

This obituary first appeared online as blog.

A poet and independent scholar, Trent Morris lives and writes in Arkansas.

———

VOYAGING WITH SEAMUS
———

Andrew O'Hagan

Into the world of light?

He was simply a source of grace, a blessing, and you always knew he was on your side. I was lucky to know those qualities and see them captured in a single name – *Seamus*. What is it about some people that they seem to carry a kind of moral gladness with them?

Not that they are always good or always right, but that they hold out the possibility of a better selfhood for everybody. In the few days since he died, I've been feeling sore in the heart, because a light has gone out, a reliable comfort. More than that: a genius with a sublime human touch is now beyond reach. I recall the story of the little boy who watched as Robert

Burns's funeral cortege passed through the town of Dumfries. "But who will be our poet now?" he said to his mother.

Two decades ago, when I worked at the *London Review of Books*, the editor, Karl Miller, would ask me to get people on the phone. Late one afternoon, when the paper was being put to bed, he had his nose about two inches from the page, a galley of Seamus's poem in tribute to Hugh MacDiarmid. "Seamus, I'm very grateful to you", said the editor to the poet down the line. "The problem is this. We're delighted with the poem, but there's a mistake in it."

("A mistake?" I imagined Seamus saying. "We can't have mistakes in the *London Review of Books*.")

"The thing is, you have this thing about MacDiarmid's 'chattering genius'. That's wrong. I'm from Scotland myself. You once said sheep chatter. And I can tell you Scottish sheep don't chatter, Seamus — they blether. Surely you mean MacDiarmid's 'blethering genius'?"

In more recent years, the three of us started going on jaunts together. Everywhere we went, Seamus was recognised, and people felt he might have made their day or changed their life. (It was part of his good nature that each claim seemed to have the same weight with him.) Three years ago, I went with him to the University of Strathclyde so that he could receive an honorary doctorate. His wife Marie and I thought he wasn't looking well and, indeed, he suffered a minor stroke before the event and was taken to the Royal Infirmary. Before the ambulance doors closed, he gave me his speech and told me to read it out. "They'll be waiting", he said. "I know you'll do some credit to the words."

When the ceremony was over and I turned up at the hospital, he was sitting up in bed, joking with Marie, while the young doctor spoke to him about how much he loved his poem "The Skunk".

My father had died at the beginning of that week. "No matter what happens", he had said to me, "make sure you go and do that thing with Seamus. He's been good to you and he's a lovely man." When I got back to Inverness, I read a poem of Seamus's at my father's funeral and dropped the poem into his grave. My father's ancestors had come to Scotland from Magherafelt — a few miles from where Seamus grew up — and it felt proper to let the poetry of the old country go with him into the stony ground. I knew both men would appreciate it, allowing neighbouring voices to bridge the day, and it gave me comfort to know that all appointments had been met.

Memory was everything to Seamus. The memory of his father digging in the yard. The memory of peeling potatoes with his mother, or once noticing the glad eye of the coalman. He had a mind to Ireland's memory, the seasonal return of faith and possibility, the falling away and the coming back of things. He cared for this the way other people care about politics. He wanted to offer value to a notion of existence beyond the bounds of sense, and that is where his language led him, to the power of wonder and miracles in daily life. Great is the friend whose one small shove can put you on the upswing. Being with him, I always felt able to give everything its due. His was a steadiness that befriended the person you wanted to be.

In Ayrshire, I once walked with him in a garden next to the town where I grew up. We took our drinks over the grass, and I showed him a gap in the trees revealing Ailsa Craig, the rock that stands in the sea between Ireland and Scotland. Later on, at the birthplace of Robert Burns, we looked in on a multimedia exhibition called the Tam O'Shanter Experience.

"Soon there'll be the Seamus Heaney Experience", said Karl Miller.

"That's right", said Seamus. "It'll be a few churns and a confessional box."

I asked Seamus how the folk around where he grew up reacted to him being awarded the Nobel prize for literature. "Ignored it for the most part, I'm sure", he said. "But yes, after the Stockholm Intervention, a certain Jackie Graham of the local grocery shop in Bellaghy wanted to open a Heaney Museum. 'It'll be good for you and good for us', he said." Seamus didn't stand in his way and made sure some manuscripts and posters were put into the fellow's hands.

We drove on and went into the old church at Ettrick, and Seamus climbed up to the pulpit. He began quoting Thomas Hardy's "The Darkling Thrush", 31 December 1900. He spoke of a visit he and Marie made to Stinsford Churchyard in Dorset, where Hardy's heart is buried, at Hogmanay in the year 2000.

"It's so quiet in here", I said. And the poet's voice rose up and seemed to rescue the beams from their own dampness. "That's a warm voice, Seamus", I said.

"Well", he replied, "the long day wanes, as the master said."

The greatest of our trips was the one to the west of Ireland. We stopped for lunch at a favourite place of Seamus's called Moran's. It specialises in oysters, and they gave us a table to ourselves in the snug. There was a nice bottle of Alsace and we all three had chowder. Seamus once wrote a poem after coming here, called "Oysters":

We had driven to that coast
Through flowers and limestone
And there we were, toasting friendship,
Laying down a perfect memory
In the cool of thatch and crockery.

Laying down a perfect memory. That was it, wasn't it? That was the thing, and I knew it at the time. In the main room of Yeats's tower at Ballylee, with the shallow stream below and the light coming at the green-framed window, I looked at Seamus and Karl and suddenly had a vision of a time when none of us would be alive.

Yeats wrote about such a feeling in his poem "In Memory of Major Robert Gregory":

Now that we're almost settled in our house
I'll name the friends that cannot sup with us ...
... Or mere companions of my youth,
All, all in my thoughts tonight being dead.

We went to the Aran Islands. As we left the boat at Inisheer, I could hear people whispering Seamus's name, and he was very good with that, saying hello to people. The island was so serene and filled with literary echoes. We climbed into a pony and trap at the pier and were soon off round the island. The man driving the vehicle was the very picture of robust outdoor health, and Seamus took pleasure, he said, in the way the fellow "lazily whipped" the pony every few seconds. "You're the famous poet", he said. He clearly thought Seamus was a country man who had made it into the universe of electricity and television.

The next day, back in Dublin, Seamus took us over to St Patrick's Cathedral, and we stood before Swift's grave, reading Yeats's tribute, then Pope's. I went round the corner from there and saw a plaque on the wall to Swift's servant – put there, apparently, by Swift himself. I thought this was very cheerfully democratic and said so to Seamus as we stood in the cathedral's main aisle. "Diligence and prudence", said Seamus. "Well played, that man."

Three winters passed before we got another journey together. We'd been thinking about Wales for some time and set out at the start of the summer in 2010. Seamus agreed that we should pick him up at a hotel near

Birmingham Airport. By the Birkenhill Parkway, Seamus was standing outside his hotel next to a fire engine, as the entire human contents of the building were evacuated in a drill. Seamus was staring into space. "Look", said Karl, "the Great Bucolic Contemplates Life Among the Ring Roads."

The landscape at the Welsh border was green and silvery and not short of magnificent, the hills rising from nowhere. Wordsworth saw a model of immortality in the hills. "Without the consciousness of a principle of immortality in the human soul", he writes in his "Essay Upon Epitaphs", "man could never have had awakened in him the desire to live in the remembrance of his fellows ... To be born and to die are the two points in which all men feel themselves to be in absolute coincidence."

The grave of the poet Henry Vaughan can be found on a hill next to the River Usk. He lies in the graveyard of Llansantffraed Church, where there are trees on every side, the trees advancing like Birnam Wood. There are words, of course, on all the graves, but more than that there are words in the air:

> They are all gone into the world of light!
> And I alone sit ling'ring here;
> Their very memory is fair and bright,
> And my sad thoughts doth clear.

Vaughan's grave is under a giant yew tree. It is stained with moss and lichens, its Latin phrases shaded. There's no obvious path up from the road, so we climbed through the grass and found the grave looking not obscure but unvisited. There's a bench to one side, with a bank of very old gravestones – some as old as Vaughan's (1695) – now attached to the wall for their preservation.

I took pictures while Karl and Seamus sat on a bench and argued about the Latin on Vaughan's grave. The epitaph speaks of maximum sin and an eternity of supplication before God. Seamus later wrote a poem where he referred to me as "ardent Andrew" and pictured him and Karl on "the mossy seat."

"Well, here's Vaughan", said Karl. "A believer. It's hard to think of you, Seamus, without belief. I find it hard not to believe you believe."

"I stopped practising a long time ago", said Seamus, "but some of it holds. If you have it as a child, it gives you a structure of consciousness – the idea there is something more."

"I probably wouldn't go that far", said Karl. "But I have to say: I always believed I would see my granny again. She was good to me."

"For me, it was my father", said Seamus. "I'd hope to see him again, all right."

We stayed there for a while and Seamus spoke about T.S. Eliot and his *Four Quartets*. In all our gadding about, there had been many versions of pastoral and an easy dalliance of time past and time present, but I sensed that, for Seamus at least, it wasn't like Eliot's rose garden up here. It was just a place where you could rest your bones, take a breath. And that's what we did that day as the world of light came into the trees.

This obituary was first published in The Guardian *on 2 September 2014.*

A novelist, essayist and critic, Andrew O'Hagan is the author of six books, most recently the fiction The Life and Opinions of Maf the Dog, and His Friend Marilyn Monroe *(Faber, 2011).*

—

TWO BOATS

—

Michael Longley

Fellow oarsmen.

I hope that one day I'll be able to write an adequate elegy for Seamus. In the meantime I offer some brief poetic reflections on my long friendship with him and Marie. At the 2011 Bloomsday conferments at University College Dublin, a number of poets were being given honorary degrees. During the formal lunch Seamus asked me, "What's the Greek for boat?" In such scholarly company I, who claim to be a translator of Homer, couldn't remember. I was mortified. Soon afterwards I wrote "Boat" as a kind of squib to ease my embarrassment, but the poem, I hope, reaches deeper than that. It anticipates Seamus's death (and my own). Marie wrote to tell me it had moved her to tears.

Six months later, having been invited to write a poem about a treasure in the National Museum, I remembered a brooch that Marie often wears.

It's modelled on the Broighter Boat, one of the most beautiful objects in the world, all sheen and intricacy, delicate as an eggshell. My poem "The Broighter Boat" is a gift for Marie. Now that Seamus has arrived in Ithaca, I want him to ease aside the stowaway and take his proper place as the "transubstantial / Imaginary oarsman."

BOAT
for Seamus

What's the Greek for boat,
You ask, old friend,
Fellow voyager
Approaching Ithaca –
Oh, flatulent sails,
Wave-winnowing oars,
Shingle-scrunching keel –
But, so close to home,
There's a danger always
Of amnesiac storms,
Waterlogged words.

THE BROIGHTER BOAT
for Marie

A friend wears as a brooch
Gold boat, golden oars,
Refinement intensified
Below her breastbone,

Mast, oars, tiller
Hammered thin as ash
Keys, sycamore wings,
Rowlocks whispering,

Her journey's replica
With me a stowaway,
A transubstantial
Imaginary oarsman.

This is an abridged version of the obituary that was first published in The Irish Times *on 7 September 2014.*

Michael Longley was the holder of the Ireland Chair of Poetry between 2007 and 2010. He is the author of 14 collections of poetry, most recently The Stairwell *(Cape, 2014). He continues to live in Belfast.*

POETRY AND TERROR

Richard Murphy

Love over terror.

(Author's Note in 2014: This review of North *was written in Cleggan, Co Galway and published in* The New York Review of Books *on 30 September 1976).*

Visitors to Ireland have often remarked that we seem to live in the past. They note our strong attachment to beliefs which were held in the Dark Ages and our inability to end a conflict which goes back to the religious wars of the seventeenth century. Our moist green landscape charms them, where it remains unpolluted by modern industry. They see fields full of cattle, which have been a source of wealth since the mythical wars of Cuchulain and Maeve. The oceanic island atmosphere takes away their sense of time, and gives them instead an illusion that the past is retrievable, perhaps even happening today. Clergy strengthen this illusion by teaching in churches and schools that the dead will be resurrected. Our earth itself, with those vast wet bogs in the center of the island, seems to absorb the present and preserve the past. Here funerals draw much larger crowds than weddings. Ruins and buried remains are so plentiful that archaeologists have an endless future digging back through time. In this climate poetry flourishes, and the poet who has shown the finest art in presenting a coherent vision of Ireland, past and present, is Seamus Heaney.

He was born on a farm in a townland called Mossbawn, near Lough Neagh between Belfast and Derry, 37 years ago, the eldest of nine children in a Catholic family. After six years at St Columb's College, run by the Diocesan priests, in Londonderry, he studied English language and literature at Queen's University in Belfast, where he began to write poetry under the spell of Gerard Manley Hopkins. His first volume, *Death of a Naturalist*, was published ten years ago in 1966. "Words as bearers of history and mystery began to invite me", he has said about this period in his life. By birth and upbringing he belonged to the ancient world of the Irish countryside and traditional culture, with roots in a pre-Christian legendary past: but his education brought him into the modern world, where he discovered English poetry. The tension you can feel in Ireland between the two cultures, you also feel in his poetry.

He is the antipode of Yeats, who extended English poetry out beyond the demesne walls into the Irish countryside to appropriate its legends. Heaney brings the Irish countryside through his own voice into English poetry.

> Those hobnailed boots from beyond the mountain
> Were walking, by God, all over the fine
> Lawns of elocution.

The result is a new and exciting sound. Granted, he has Irish antecedents – Patrick Kavanagh, for example – and granted, he has learned the craft of being true to his own Irish voice from a number of English and American poets, such as Edward Thomas, Robert Frost and Ted Hughes. His original power, which even the sternest critics bow to with respect, is that he can give you the feeling as you read his poems that you are actually doing what they describe. His words not only mean what they say, they sound like their meaning. Often in his early poems he celebrates hard physical work, such as digging, bulling cows, ditching, ploughing, catching eels: all kinds of activities associated with ancient rural crafts and fertility which he witnessed as a child, a dead life which his poetry resurrects in a living body of words. His work has the potent charm of bringing back an old kind of beauty and a numinous fear, which cruder industrial terrors have all but blotted out: and it celebrates the newly discovered force of the poetic craft itself.

His primary statement about this craft, in the opening lines of his first book, connects poetry with terror.

> Between my finger and my thumb
> The squat pen rests, snug as a gun.

Bullfrogs are compared to "mud grenades", and butter crocks on a pantry shelf to "large pottery bombs." Even allowing for the fashion in the sixties for overemphasizing the toughness and cruelty of nature, you feel that these images are true. Grenades and bombs *were* kept on some remote Irish farms during his childhood. So aptly in "The Barn",

> The musty dark hoarded an armoury
> Of farmyard implements, harness, plough-socks.

Heaney's second volume, *Door into the Dark*, appeared in 1969, the year when violence in Northern Ireland became world news. For three years he remained in Belfast, living with his wife and two sons in a "Protestant" street near the university where he taught. On the corner of this road a pub and its owner were blown up. Poetry that can digest this kind of horror is rare, though horror of this kind has produced much ill-digested poetry.

In 1972 he published his third collection, *Wintering Out*, which confirmed his gradual inward emigration into a new world of language.

> The tawny guttural water
> spells itself: Moyola
> is its own score and consort,
>
> bedding the locale
> in the utterance,
> reed music, an old chanter
>
> breathing its mists
> through vowels and history.

Four years ago he moved south across the border with his family to live in a cottage on the edge of the Wicklow Mountains; choosing to become "an inner émigré", like the Russian poets Mandelstam, Akhmatova and Pasternak. Heaney defines this role at the end of *North*, in "Exposure":

> I am neither internee nor informer;
> An inner émigré, grown long-haired
> And thoughtful: a wood-kerne
>
> Escaped from the massacre,
> Taking protective colouring
> From bole and bark, feeling
> Every wind that blows

"The fear that goes with the writing of verse", says Nadezhda Mandelstam in *Hope Against Hope*, "has nothing in common with the fear one experiences in the presence of the secret police. Our mysterious awe in the face of existence itself is always overridden by the more primitive fear of violence and destruction. M[andelstam] often spoke of how the first kind of fear had disappeared with the Revolution that had shed so much blood before our eyes."

Seamus Heaney brings both kinds of fear together – the creative awe and the destructive horror – connecting the brutal real atrocities we have been shown on television for the past seven years with rituals of human sacrifice in remote antiquity. His poetry traces modern terrorism back to its roots in the early Iron Age, and mysterious awe back to the "bonehouse" of language itself. He looks closely in *North* at our funeral rites and our worship of the past. The whole of northern civilization from Denmark to Donegal is his "locale." We hear of Thor and Gunnar as well as Hercules: the Vikings as well as Sir Walter Raleigh. The central image of this work, a symbol which unifies time, person, and place, is bogland: it contains, preserves, and yields up terror as well as awe.

The nature of peat is to preserve certain things that are buried in it: primeval forests, elks, butter, suicides, strangled victims. In a lecture called "Feeling into Words", addressed to the Royal Society of Literature in London on October 17, 1974, Heaney said:

> I began to get an idea of bog as the memory of the landscape, or as a landscape that remembered everything that happened in and to it. In fact, if you go round the National Museum in Dublin, you will realize that a great proportion of the most cherished material heritage of Ireland was "found in a bog."

He went on to say that he "had been reading about the frontier and the west as an important myth in the American consciousness, so I set up – or rather, laid down – the bog as an answering Irish myth." This is the conclusion of his poem "Bogland", at the end of *Door into the Dark*:

> Our pioneers keep striking
> Inwards and downwards,
>
> Every layer they strip
> Seems camped on before.
> The bogholes might be Atlantic seepage.
> The wet centre is bottomless.

Heaney's original idea of bogland as a symbol of memory was objectively confirmed and extended by both political event and archaeological discovery. In 1969 the civil-rights marches in the city of Derry, and the counter-marches by the Royal Ulster Constabulary with batons drawn, focused world attention on the Catholics who lived in a low-lying slum called the Bogside. In a short while the word became synonymous for minority resistance to police oppression, and subsequently Irish Catholic resistance to British misrule. Bog itself is one of the few words of Irish origin to have been assimilated into English. Literally it means "soft". In English it acquired, perhaps because of its Irish origin as well as its color, connotations of shame, as in the slang of "bog" meaning "lavatory". Heaney carries the word up the ladder from the foul rag and boneshop to give it a nobler meaning. He was helped by publication in 1969 of *The Bog People* by the Danish archaeologist P.V. Glob.

What this fascinating book meant to him is best described in Heaney's own words.

> It was chiefly concerned with preserved bodies of men and women found in the bogs of Jutland, naked, strangled or with their throats cut, disposed under the peat since early Iron Age times ... P.V. Glob argues convincingly that a number of these, and in particular, the Tollund Man, whose head is now preserved near Aarhus in the museum at Silkeborg, were ritual sacrifices to the Mother Goddess, the goddess of the ground who needed new bridegrooms each winter to bed with her in her sacred place, in the bog, to ensure the renewal and fertility of the territory in the spring. Taken in relation to the tradition of Irish political martyrdom for the cause whose icon is Kathleen Ni Houlihan, this is more than an archaic barbarous rite: it is an archetypal pattern. And the unforgettable photographs of these victims blended in my mind with photographs of atrocities, past and present, in the long rites of Irish political and religious struggles.

Heaney first made a connection between these Danish murders of two thousand years ago and modern Irish politics in a powerful poem called "The Tollund Man" in *Wintering Out*. Now in *North* he has created a cycle of six or more bog-sacrifice poems, compressing the archaeological information given by Glob into personal imagery. You could call them love poems that resurrect the dead in poetry. The language, like seed, is compact with life, sexual, even necrophiliac.

I reach past
The riverbed's washed
Dream of gold to the bullion
Of her Venus bone.

You can feel the joy as well as the terror of ancient rites, a victim "hung in
the scales / with beauty and atrocity", whose spine is "an eel arrested / under
a glisten of mud." Sometimes the poet assumes a victim's identity, as in "Bog
Queen", who speaks of her burial and resurrection in the first person: "My
skull hibernated / in the wet nest of my hair." The short lines, the seminal
images, and the vast connections in time or space between fragile details
build up in "Kinship" (a six-page poem in six movements), which begins with
a figure of circles: neck, nest, and a dog's motion before lying down.

Kinned by hieroglyphic
peat on a spreadfield
to the strangled victim,
the love-nest in the bracken,

I step through origins
like a dog turning
its memories of wilderness
on the kitchen mat:

Many dead words are revived. From Old English and Norse he digs up
bonehouse from *banhus* meaning body; *scop* meaning poet; and *holmgang*, a
duel to the death. Irish words are slipped in, like foreign coins in a meter:
crannog, an ancient lake dwelling; *aisling*, a vision: *bawn*, a ringed mound or
fort: *slobland*, a marsh. He brings out refined shades of meaning in verbal
sounds. "Dublin" is "spined and plosive." Remembering the laid-out corpses
of the dead in his childhood, he recalls "their dough-white hands / shackled
in rosary beads." The dead subject, the dead past, is described in language
that's vividly alive: a grim statement in a joyful style. The "swimming
tongue" of a Viking longship is "buoyant with hindsight", and the final
message of this tongue to Ireland in the future is:

Keep your eye clear
as the bleb of the icicle,

trust the feel of what nubbed treasure
your hands have known.

Heaney has said that "the bog bank is a memory bank." How does it store and yield information? The symbol suggests that the past is continuously present under the ground we tread, permanently preserved, static and dead. It also suggests that no improving human change is possible, because all action is absorbed by the soft wet ground forever. Digging up the past, or writing poetry, appears to be the only way of redemption or renewal: a kind of resurrection. The symbol conveys a profound truth about Irish consciousness, and how we keep the past alive. But the bog has *not* "remembered everything that happened in and to it." Most of what happened has been forgotten. A few sacred objects congenial to itself are preserved by its acids: and what the peat yields up when the poet digs down deep enough is a strangled victim or a severed head. The bog does not liberate us with new knowledge of accurate history: it horrifies us with timeless myths perpetuating acts of cruelty based upon errors of judgment.

The dreadful power of the symbol is generated by the poetry with fascination amounting to approval. The poems embody the myths. In other poems, such as "Ocean's Love to Ireland", the vision is more historical. In "Act of Union" Heaney imagines the relationship between England and Ireland in the past as the rape of a feminine land by a male imperial power. No attempt here to demythologize the past. As in the bog poems — significantly it begins with an image of the bog — it acts like the peat itself, converting history into myth.

Are these images of human sacrifice redemptive in the sense that tragedy can be? I think this poetry is seriously attempting to purge our land of a terrible blood-guilt, and inwardly acknowledging our enslavement to a sacrificial myth. I think it may go a long way toward freeing us from the myth by portraying it in its true archaic shape and color, not disguising its brutality. Naturally we wonder where Heaney himself stands in relation to the victims and the killers, what he has called "the tail end of a struggle in a province between territorial piety and imperial power." He makes no pretense about his deep uncertainty. *Incertus* was once a pseudonym he used. Some of his poems are "trial pieces", and they follow a thought "like a child's tongue following the toils of his calligraphy."

Heaney looks for companions in literature. He's both resourceful and protean. His ear is always to the ground from which, like Antaeus, he draws his strength. He converses with historical or literary figures, Breughel or Hamlet. Does he approve of Diodorus Siculus in a poem called "Strange Fruit", about a "girl's head like an exhumed gourd"? This puzzled me until I found in my battered ninth edition of the *Encyclopaedia Britannica* that Diodorus Siculus "as a critic ... seems to have been altogether ignorant of the ethical advantages of history, and shrinks from administering praise or blame to the persons whose history he writes." So too Heaney's detachment could be a necessary element in the purification of our guilt.

Although Heaney commits himself to no belief in the causes that might claim his allegiance, such as the unification of Ireland, he embodies in poetry some of the terrorist actions that he refuses to endorse; as in a frightening poem called "Punishment", about the penalties inflicted in ancient Jutland and modern Belfast on girls who might have misbehaved. There is much sad truth in that evasive word "almost" in this passage:

My poor scapegoat,

I almost love you
but would have cast, I know,
the stones of silence.

At the end of "Kinship" he addresses Tacitus, who reported with urbane critical accuracy the custom of human sacrifice among the barbarous Germani, and tells him he has found "a desolate peace." This involves self-lacerating recognition, *almost* rejection, of the goddess, whose victims are in other poems treated as "holy blissful martyrs", their bodies preserved like those of the saints. The repulsion in these lines is far from Yeats's vision of the terrible beauty born in the sacrifice of Easter 1916, and closer to Joyce's:

Our mother ground
is sour with the blood
of her faithful,

they lie gargling
in her sacred heart
as the legions stare
from the ramparts.

Come back to this
"island of the ocean"
where nothing will suffice.
Read the inhumed faces

of casualty and victim;
report us fairly,
how we slaughter
for the common good

and shave the heads
of the notorious,
how the goddess swallows
our love and terror.

To bring together things, feelings, and ideas in words which have never before been connected is imagination of the highest kind; and in this rare quality Seamus Heaney's *North* excels. I read it as a triumph of art over terror. It has the fear of death on almost every page, and brings the terror under artistic control. The book's weakness is confined to a small section at the end, added like a print-room to a gallery of paintings. Here the poems are lower-keyed, more talkative. The verse is looser, the language and imagery are not so inspired.

Terror darkens this book, but the poem which has the last word appears as a frontispiece. Every word in it rings true to the culture, to my memory of Ireland in the past, to its sad beauty. The play of light and shadow in this poem, the spaces filled by sunlight, the woman baking bread, the tick of two clocks work like a revelation as in the art of Vermeer. I'm thinking of the *Officer and Laughing Girl* at the Frick, where a dark moment of time is suspended forever in a ray of light that pours through an open window, crosses a blank wall under a map of Holland, and is caught up by a girl's ecstatic smile. Heaney's poem is called "Mossbawn: Sunlight", after his birthplace.

There was a sunlit absence.
The helmeted pump in the yard
heated its iron,
water honeyed

in the slung bucket
and the sun stood
like a griddle cooling
against the wall

of each long afternoon.
So, her hands scuffled
over the bakeboard,
the reddening stove

sent its plaque of heat
against her where she stood
in a floury apron
by the window.

Now she dusts the board
with a goose's wing,
now sits, broad-lapped,
with whitened nails

and measling shins:
here is a space
again, the scone rising
to the tick of two clocks.

And here is love
like a tinsmith's scoop
sunk past its gleam
in the meal-bin.

Richard Murphy was born in Co Mayo in 1927. He attended both Magdalen College Oxford and the Sorbonne. The author of six individual collections, as well as selected editions, his most volume of poetry is The Pleasure Ground: Poems 1952–2012 *(Bloodaxe, 2014). He currently lives in Sri Lanka.*

HEWITT ON ULSTER

President Michael D. Higgins

A new concept of unity.

Is í seo an chéad deis a bhí agam teacht go hArd Mhacha mar Uachtarán na hÉireann. Táim, dar ndóigh, ar an eolas maidir leis an mbreithiúnas machnamhach a thug Aodh de Blácam, iriseoir Éireannach sna 1930idí, ar Ard Mhacha, nuair a thug sé cathair gheanúil air agus a dúirt: "fair in its site, its sacred buildings and homes of learning, its air of quietude, culture and ease."

(This is my first opportunity to come to Armagh as President of Ireland. I am of course very aware of the reflective assessment given to it in the 1930s by Aodh de Blácam, an Irish journalist who called Armagh a lovable city, "fair in its site, its sacred buildings and homes of learning, its air of quietude, culture and ease.")

I approach the subject of John Hewitt, his life, work and legacy with some trepidation in a "region", as he would put it, that is so leavened by the poetic instinct that humility from such as myself is more of a necessity than a suggestion.

As I am about to speak in tribute to one who was so well aware of the appalling waste of life that is war, and a writer of conscience who kept returning to the ethics of his internationalism, I am also conscious that the circumstances of violent loss of life in which I am speaking are ones that would not only break his heart, as they are breaking the heart of many, but also force his pen.

Allow me then just a few words on those present circumstances. I believe that the enormous increase in unsettled conflicts at the present time represents a great challenge to the international community. It also represents a great failure. It surely must be a matter of profound concern to citizens across the globe and their heads of state and leaders that so many conflicts – in Gaza, Syria, Iraq, Ukraine and elsewhere – have endured to the point where loss of life is now increasing on a daily basis, security is decreasing, and refugee numbers are escalating as displacement drives on relentlessly with horrific consequences on the most vulnerable. It is a time when we are challenged to innovate in the search for peace, realising that a status quo of unacknowledged failure within a diplomacy of narrow interests, and compounded by the consequences of diplomatic failure, is threatening all of our human achievements.

The appalling and escalating loss of life in Gaza is a tragic example of the failure of diplomacy. There is an awareness among our citizens of the importance of building and securing peaceful resolution to such conflicts, which challenge us all. In recent weeks, I have received a great volume of correspondence from members of the public expressing their horror at what is happening in Gaza and I share their horror at the perceived failure of language itself, as I know you do. In celebrating the life and work of John Hewitt – one who cared so deeply about peace and the relations between peoples – it is wholly appropriate that we reflect on the relevance and resonance of Hewitt's work in the atmosphere of today's conflicts; and I could not speak with authenticity here today without making reference to these events.

In preparation for my speech today I read, *inter alia*, Peter McDonald's assessment of John Hewitt in the *Oxford Handbook of Modern Irish Poetry*, in which he remarks that, in a way, John Hewitt dead has been far more influential than John Hewitt the living writer. This view is no doubt influenced by the fact that he is now a subject of that most potent form of Irish commemoration – the literary and academic summer school – and I wish to acknowledge my debt, in presenting these remarks, to Frank Ormsby's magnificent introduction to the *Collected Poems of John Hewitt*, and to such fine memoir pieces as that of Patricia Craig in a recent edition of the incomparable *Irish Pages*, which I read regularly.

What an excellent programme you have for this week, with one of Ireland's leading poets, a dazzling prose writer and memoirist, John Montague, as one of the speakers at this summer school. I will be reflecting briefly on some of the connections John Hewitt made with John Montague and how these connections have given us greater insight into the meaning of Hewitt's work.

When I visited Coventry as part of my state visit to the United Kingdom earlier this year, I met many Irish emigrants who were amongst the half a million Irish men and women who travelled to England in the 1950s to work on the construction sites, in the hospitals and schools, and in so many other sectors of economy and society. I found it a joy to be able to celebrate the fact that there is virtually no aspect of British civic or political life that has not been enriched by the Irish community. I was pleased to bear witness to their contribution to the culture and life of Britain, and, in turn, to their continuing contribution, as migrants and people of new shores, to the renewal of our own Irish identity.

Of course, Coventry received a very special emigrant from these shores in the 1950s when John Hewitt left Northern Ireland to take up the position of director of the Herbert Art Gallery and Museum. It was while there, from what was a bittersweet exile, that he wrote many of his most thoughtful and resonant poems, including "An Irishman in Coventry" which he composed the year after he moved to that city. It ends with the words:

> Yet like Lir's children, banished to the waters,
> Our hearts still listen for the landward bells.

It is interesting to reflect on how Hewitt's sense of identity seems to have changed on his move to Coventry. He was an Ulsterman in Northern Ireland but an Irishman in England. Hewitt of course gave the issues of identity and memory a great deal of reflection. In an article in *The Belfast Telegraph* in 1958 he wrote:

> In the heart of the English midlands looking back from the fulcrum
> of middle age on my personal adventures among those books
> which were a significant part of my Irish past, I sometimes wonder
> if time and distance have given me a perspective and objectivity or
> if sentiment and the ordinary wear and tear of memory may not
> have distorted details and proportion.

Hewitt's vision of Ulster included a multitude of identities competing for space. His "Ulsterman" was part:

> Kelt, Briton, Saxon, Dane, and Scot,
> Time and this island tied a crazy knot.

But categories and their naming should not obscure from us the gift of a father's egalitarian thought that would endure for life as a legacy, one that might, as Frank Ormsby tells us, have led to his youthful borrowing of ten shillings from his mother to buy a second-hand five-volume set of William Morris's *The Earthly Paradise*.

Hewitt said of his poem "The Colony" that it was the definitive statement of his realization that he was an Ulsterman. In this poem, Hewitt conjured the point of view of a Roman colonizer in England in the historic period when the Roman Empire itself was in decline. Edna Longley has declared this poem a "sophisticated poetic model of Ulster politics."

The *Irish Times* used its closing line, "we shall not be outcast on the world", for the title of an editorial responding to an initiative of British Prime Minister Edward Heath in 1972 that would result in the Sunningdale Agreement later that year. The editor argued that the majority in Northern Ireland now had a chance to prove that they are in their right place, and wrote, "In the words of their own poet, John Hewitt, the Northern majority will be able to say: 'We would be strangers in the Capitol; This is our country also, no-where else; And we shall not be outcast on the world'."

Hewitt was very forthright in invoking and declaring his planter identity and heritage. Indeed, as part of a literary tour in 1970, he jointly published with John Montague the poetry collection *The Planter and the Gael*, with each poet contributing work from their respective viewpoints and both being very aware of their representative status. In his introduction to this collection, Michael Longley wrote:

> Each poet explores his experience of Ulster, the background in which he grew up and the tradition which has shaped his work. John Montague defines the culture of the Gael, John Hewitt that of the Planter. The two bodies of work complement each other and provide illuminating insight into the cultural complexities of the Province.

The integrity of both poets, Hewitt and Montague, and Longley too, is reflected in their rejection of any accommodating amnesia as to the complex past.

A study from the 1970s of the use of landscape in *The Planter and the Gael* by John Wilson Foster pointed clearly to how the land and landscape are called up through the different backgrounds of Montague and Hewitt. The poems of Montague reflect loss, decay, absence and exile, whereas Hewitt views the land through a planter's sensibility, one of invoking the human labour expended on it, the memory of harnessing its fertility, husbanding it and taming it for productive use. This legacy constitutes an invocation of Irishness. For Hewitt, his identity was bound up in place and landscape. Another such example of Hewitt's connection to the landscape can be seen in his poem "Townland of Peace". There is here, I believe, a claim for a sovereignty of sensory intimacy, an intimacy not appropriately mediated by either the ideological abuse of memory or a limiting pursuit of respectability.

Perhaps the most resonant example of Hewitt's understanding of the complex identity faced by those in Northern Ireland is contained in his essay "Planter's Gothic: An Essay in Discursive Autobiography". In this work, Hewitt discussed his reaction to a Planter's Gothic tower built on the remains of a round tower. Discussing its impact on him, he wrote:

> It is the best symbol I have found for the strange textures of my response to this island of which I am a native. It may appear Planter's Gothic, but there is a round tower somewhere inside, and needled through every sentence I utter.

As well as this multifaceted understanding of identity that he recognized as existing in Northern Ireland, Hewitt was also very aware of the wider connection of the region which he regarded as home (and about which he wrote so frequently) to Europe. In an introduction to a catalogue for an art exhibition taking place in Belfast, he expanded:

> At the beginning of the last century Belfast was in full contact with the flow of European events. But in the intervening period, mainly for political-economic reasons, the scope of wit and culture suffered a time-lag of increasing proportions. Our province became provincial. However, since the Great War and partly consequent upon it, the acceleration of social change has narrowed the gap between Ulster and Europe. Once again our best aesthetic thought is coloured by contemporary tendencies.

Hewitt himself spent time in Europe. The Public Record Office of Northern Ireland holds his notebooks, which contain detailed accounts of his educational holidays in Europe. As they wryly note, because of his egalitarian sympathies, he was naturally attracted to Russia and countries such as Czechoslovakia, East Germany, Hungary, Poland and Yugoslavia. Consideration of how the materialist and statist excesses – changing a utopian vision into dystopia, in the communal response to the abuses of empire in such places, and how this affected John Hewitt – will have to await another day.

Hewitt was always very insistent that the placement of his home region into the wider continental context was vital and that missing out any element of the broader picture would lead to profound misunderstandings. In a letter to John Montague he asserted:

> I always maintained that our loyalties had an order: to Ulster, to Ireland, to the British Archipelago, to Europe; and that anyone who skipped a step or missed a link falsified the total. The Unionists missed out Ireland: the Northern Nationalists (The Green Tories) couldn't see the Ulster under their feet; the Republicans missed out both Ulster and the Archipelago; and none gave any heed to Europe at all. Now, perhaps, willy nilly bundled in the European rump of the Common Market, clearer ideas of our regional and national allegiances and responsibilities may emerge, or our whole sad stubborn conglomeration of nations may founder and disappear for ever.

Such views on the opportunity that Europe presented to Northern Ireland were very close to the thinking of the Swiss philosopher Denis de Rougemont. Rougemont, a member of the Personalist movement, was a committed European who saw that Europe after the Second World War needed a new concept of unity. He looked to the regional model, to the principle of subsidiarity, and also to the origins of the continent and its founding myths. For him, Homer's stories of the *Iliad* and the *Odyssey* were more relevant than the nation state for understanding the future of Europe. Indeed, for Rougemont, *the ultimate foundation of our European identity is not the national state at all, but the European unity represented by our shared cultural roots*. The ancient myths that we, along with the other peoples of Europe, have as the foundations of our literatures provide us with a shared vision but also a respect for cultural diversity. Invocation of myths and their influence on the progress of Europe is not, however, to make a hegemonic claim or, much worse, to create an undertone of assertion as to origins. Our founding myths are universal and their traces are in the diverse locations of the wisdoms in the world, in all of our faith systems.

I think that Rougemont was very perceptive in his insights that a shared influence of myths and cultural memory intangibly links us all together in Europe. Yet it is neither the exclusive, nor the sufficient, reflection of the intellectual roots of our sensibility. The categories of both memory and imagination must always remain open.

A further example of such sensibility is seen in a poet who was a contemporary of Hewitt in the Belfast Group – Michael Longley. On the eve of the IRA's ceasefire in 1994, Longley had been working on a poem based on an extract from the *Iliad*. He sent a copy of the finished work to John Banville, then literary editor of the *Irish Times*. Recognising the quality and meaning of the work, Banville "stopped the presses" and ensured its inclusion in the paper in the same week as the ceasefire was declared. The poem is based on the episode in the *Iliad* which tells the story of Priam, the King of Troy and Achilles, the Greek warrior who killed his son Hector. I have quoted the words Michael Longley gave Priam more than once:

I get down on my knees and do what must be done
And kiss Achilles' hand, the killer of my son.

One cannot but be struck by the generosity, empathy and remorse that are reflected in these words by Longley, rooted as they are in a poem that has its origins nearly 3,000 years ago. Longley's words echo back through the millennia to Homer, and forward to today with immediacy and power. Troy was not saved by the gesture. The moral intention in the action and the words, however, has its own sustaining power beyond succeeding circumstances. It is appropriate for us to remember Hannah Arendt's suggestion that, to have authentic meaning, forgiveness must be aimed at either preventing or enabling future events, events over which all must have influence.

Denis de Rougemont coined the phrase "a Europe of the regions." He suggested that it was necessary to leave behind arid concepts of territorial divisions and instead consider the interdependent relationships that all communities experience. For him, the key thing was to allow human communities to cooperate in very practical ways and he was particularly interested in trans-boundary regions which, he felt, would be in the vanguard in teaching the rest of Europe how to order itself. He considered that it was only by overcoming divisions that we would preserve our diversity.

For Hewitt, concepts of the region and regionalism were themes that he engaged with through his prose work and his poetry. His vision of regionalism began with a revival of the poetry of peace and feeling and its language. He worked throughout his life to promote the regional culture of Ulster as a distinct identity. In "Townland of Peace" he averred:

> But these small rights require a smaller stage
> than the vast forum of the nations' rage
> for they imply a well-compacted space
> where every voice recalls its nation's place,
> townland, townquarter, county at its most …

Hewitt was of the view that:

> Ulster considered as a Region and not as a symbol of any particular creed, can command the loyalty of every one of its inhabitants. For regional identity does not preclude, rather it requires, membership of a larger association. And whatever that association may be … there should emerge a culture and an attitude individual and distinctive … and no mere echo of the thought and imagination of another people or another land.

This is both a suggestion and a recognition of the importance of a rooted imagination – a multi-rooted, uninhibited, generous imagination.

Culture can play an enormous role in reinvigorating the wider society. I had the opportunity when I was Minister for Culture during Ireland's presidency of the EU in 1996 to oversee a key piece of legislation that focussed on the integration of cultural aspects into community actions. It affirmed that access to culture and the expression of cultural identity were essential conditions for the full participation of citizens in society. In this current period of high unemployment, with its related insecurities and poverty, as we pursue a sustainable economic recovery, we must not lose sight of the key path that culture offers in helping us reclaim a flourishing and ethical role in the wider global community.

Hewitt's views on regionalism also bring to mind the ideas of the French theorist and philosopher Paul Ricoeur. In his work, Ricoeur posed the question as to how one might be modern and yet continue tradition, how we might revive an old dormant civilization as part of universal civilization. He understood that it was not easy to remain radically and authentically personal, and at the same time practise tolerance towards other civilizations. As he saw it, the discovery of the plurality of cultures is never a harmless experience. So how is an encounter with different cultures possible when understanding the other can seem such a dangerous venture, that could result in the loss of your own cultural heritage? Paul Ricoeur's own answer to this question was that a culture had to engage with what had preceded it, what is occurring around it, and what flows from it.

In this consideration of regionalism and of what Ulster means, Seamus Heaney too had a perceptive insight:

Each person in Ulster lives first in the Ulster of the actual present, and then in one or other Ulster of the mind.

Hewitt saw the different traditions as interrelated and he felt the best way to recognize the reconciling implications of this was at the regional level. For Hewitt, the region was small enough to garner the kind of loyalty which is needed to transcend differences.

The region could also act as a counter-weight to what he saw as the prevailing forces of over-centralization. He based this view on his conviction that we must, as social beings, facing the enormously complicated structure that is the modern nation state, find some smaller unit to which to give our loyalty. He saw this as a necessary precondition that could then lead to economic invigoration of regional agriculture and industry.

His views on the importance of developing a regional outlook can also be seen as his reaction to the impact of partition on Northern Ireland. His hopes of the development of a regional loyalty were, of course, stymied by the Troubles. But now that we have emerged from that dark period, there is an opportunity to revisit and draw inspiration from Hewitt's ideas of regionalism. In this context, I am struck particularly by the recent analysis of the 2011 census results by the Northern Ireland Statistics and Research Agency. For the first time, the census has started to ask questions about national identity. Particularly striking was that, when asked for the first time how they viewed their own national identity, 29% of the people included Northern Irish as a part of that identity: something new is emerging here.

Hewitt's reflections and understanding of these complex questions — regionalism and identity — are relevant in grasping the situation that currently exists in Northern Ireland, and how people see themselves in the context of their wider allegiances to Ireland and the UK. People are perhaps now more comfortable in endorsing multiple identities that suit the shifting way in which we, as individuals, relate to a world that is increasingly fluid and porous, one that we must struggle beyond boundaries and states to make accountable and sustainable.

We must take into consideration, too, the new community of immigrants in Northern Ireland with more than 120,000 arriving between 2000 and 2010. To quote an Assembly paper, "there is little doubt that the inflow of new residents from countries as far apart as Poland, Brazil and East Timor, has enriched the culture and society of Northern Ireland." It will be fascinating to hear from those migrants how they view their own identity changing, as they respond to what they are making their new home region – and also to see what their responses will be to the national identity question at the next census in 2021, and beyond.

May I, to conclude, repeat how Hewitt was a man who understood that we all are the carriers of multiple allegiances, multiple identities, empowered by hopes and ideas yet to be realized? John Hewitt understood that, to find peace, he needed to know his own place in the world. His lifelong work was to understand himself and his place – his identity, his culture, his region – in order to achieve an understanding of the self and the world; and he informed it all with an inherited respect for the power and potential of an emancipatory egalitarianism. These existential reflections rooted a moral and utopian instinct, and remain as valid and as valuable now, as they did when Hewitt first considered them.

So it is with great gratitude and respect that I grant him the final word from "Townland of Peace", his powerful evocation of personal memory and the intimacy of peace:

> Now and for ever through the change-rocked years,
> I know my corner in the universe;
> My corner, this small region limited
> In space by sea, in the time by my own dead ...

This address was delivered at the John Hewitt Summer School, Market Place Theatre, Armagh on 28 August, 2014.

A poet as well as a politician, Michael D. Higgins is the ninth President of Ireland. He served as a Labour TD in Dáil Éireann for 25 years, including as Minister for the Arts, Culture and the Gaeltacht. His fourth collection of poems is New and Selected Poems *(Liberties Press, 2011).*

DÁN

—

Nuala Ní Dhomhnaill

IN MEMORIAM SÉAMUS HEANEY

Faoi mar a thitfeadh crann mór
i lár na foraoise an turlabhait
a dhein sé nuair a thit sé
do chualathas insa Domhan Thoir é.
Chualamairne féin an tuairt
cé go rabhamar i bhfad ó bhaile
is thuigeamar láithreach, is ar an dtoirt,
go raibh rí na coille ar lár.

Is faoi mar a dúirt Eibhlín Dubh fadó
is ar ár gcroí bhí cumha
ná leigheasfadh Cúige Mumhan
ná gaibhne Oileán na bhFionn.
Dob é ár mbuachaill beo é
ár nGile Mear, ár rogha, ár bpíobaire.
Do sheinn sé suas is bhagair sinn
go dtí Tír Tairngre.

IN MEMORIAM SEAMUS HEANEY

Just as if a tree fell in the heart
of the forest. The crashing sound
it made could be heard
all the way to the Eastern World.
We too heard the commotion
though we were far from home
and we understood at once, and on the spot
the the King of the Forest was felled.

And as Eileen Dubh said long ago
in our hearts was a torn hole
of grief that could not be filled
by all the wide expanse of Munster
or the wordsmiths of that fair island
that is Ireland.
He was our likely lad, our Giolla Mear,
our piper, our chosen one.
He piped us on and led us in
to the Promised Land.

Translated by the author.

Nuala Ní Dhomhnaill is one of Ireland's most celebrated poets. Her latest collection is The
Fifty-Minute Mermaid *(The Gallery Press, 2007).*

LUAS

Pascal Mac Gabhann

Lá 'le Bríde, nuair a shíneann sé a chosa thar cholpa
na leapa, braitheann Aodh, easpag scortha, braitheann sé
luas is léim ann féin, luasc an earraigh ag corraí ina ghéaga.
Sin uile in ainneoin an cheithre scóir a bheith slánaithe aige.

"Ar an Líne Uaine a thabharfad m'aghaidh", ar sé i dtuin
chainte a cuireadh cantaireacht Ghreagórach i gcuimhne duit.
Léimeann John Charles, an peata cait, de chos na leapa, ligeann
scréach as agus greadann leis amach an fhuinneog oscailte

san árasán íoslaigh i gCearnóg Mhic Liam. Fanann John Charles
lasmuigh ag amharc isteach ar Aodh. "Is é Gleann Bhríde ceann
scríbe m'oilithreachta inniu", a deir Aodh, é ag caint leis féin,
is dóichí, mar níl peacach ar bith ná baistíoch beo eile laistigh

de na ceithre bhalla mar a mhaireann an t-easpag. A dhroim
le ráillí Fhaiche Stiabhna, fanann Aodh le ceann de thramanna
Luais, an córas iarnród sráide. Ó am go ham amharcann sé ó dheas
go bhfeiceann faoi dheireadh an smut glioscarnach ag déanamh

ar an ardán. Liúnn Aodh amach in ard a ghutha: "Tá siad ag teacht."
Ní thugtar puinn airde ar a aistíl iompair agus ní thuigtear pioc
den tagairt Artúraíoch. Sleamhnaíonn an tram isteach de luas
maolaithe ciúin. Lena phas taistil ina láimh bordálann an t-easpag

scortha an tram úrscothach. Is sanas cogair Aodh anois i ngluais.
Imíonn sé gan cheist le sruth an Luais. Ar luas a chuid anála féin a
thugann sé iomlán a airde. Anáil ar anáil síothlaíonn an deannaíl
agus an griofadach a phiardálann a ghéaga ó am go chéile le blianta

beaga anuas. Ar an láthair bheo a dhíríonn Aodh é féin. Tugann
sé iomlán a shuntais do ghlór séimh na mná a ghlaonn amach
na stopanna, ceann ar cheann: Sráid Fhearchair, Charlemont,
Raghnallach, Coill na Feá, Cowper, Baile an Mhuilinn. Téann sé

rite ar Aodh fáil réidh le Coill na Feá. Rothlaíonn an logainm
timpeall agus timpeall i ndroma níocháin a aigne. Ach fós féin agus
é ag iomrascáil le claonta a nádúir, coinníonn Aodh greim an tsiosúir
ar an am i láthair. Déanann an t-easpag scortha, a sheacht ndícheall

a bheith i láthair na huaire ach tosaíonn glór paiteanta na mná
agus ainmneacha na stopanna, tosaíonn siad ag macallú ina cheann
cipín liath: Na Glasáin, Dún Droma, Baile Amhlaoibh, Cill Mochuda,
Stigh Lorgan, Áth an Ghainimh, An Pháirc Láir, Gleann an Chairn,

An Eachrais. Feadh an ama seo bíonn paisnéirí ag bordáil
is paisnéirí ag fágáil, paisnéirí ag labhairt os ard ar a bhfóin phóca,
paisnéirí ag téacsáil, paisnéirí eile agus cluasáin orthu ag éisteacht
le ceol. Ceann riain difriúil ag mórán acu agus glór paiteanta na mná

ag meabhrú dóibh cá bhfuil siad agus cá bhfuil a dtriallta scoir,
Gleann Bhaile na Lobhar, Coill Bhaile Uí Ógáin, Carraig Mhaighin,
Baile an Locháin, Coill na Silíní. Ar strae i bhforaois an easpa céille
tá mearadh ar Aodh agus eitlíonn sé i mbarra na gcraobh chomh scaipthe

le Suibhne Gealt. Idir Coill na Silíní agus Gleann Bhríde titeann a chodladh
air.
Ní leagann sé cos ar *terra firma* go bhfilleann an tram ar Fhaiche Stiabhna.

Born in 1946 in Crosserlough, Co Cavan, Pascal Mac Gabhann attended St Patrick's College, Maynooth and University College, Dublin. He subsequently worked for many years as a teacher at second and third levels. His single collection of poems, Sciatháin Chéaracha *(An Clóchomhar), appeared in 1979. He has continued to write poetry, and is currently working on his next collection. He lives in Dublin.*

AS SUIBHNE /
FROM SWEENEY, AN INTERTONGUING

Rody Gorman

AN TOBAR ÚD THALL / THAT WELL OVER BY
i.m. *Seamus Heaney 1939–2013*

Teorainn

Sin teorainn do chille
I do chríoch is i d'fhearann
I nDál Araidhe ceart go leor —
Cé ar bith cén rí buile
A thiocfadh aniar aduaidh ort mar sin,
A éarlaimh uasail, a fhir comhalta tiomna,
A fhir mhín mhuinteartha,
Seasfaidh gach ar leag tú síos
Mar a bhfuil guth do chloig le clos
Fós go deo na ndeor.

Boundaries

That's the boundaries of your churchyardcell in your endboundland and
quarterland-domain in Dalnaria right enough — whatever mad king might
come on you unawares like that so, noble patron, keeper of the covenant,
gentle and genial man, everything you set down where the voice-sound of
your blisterclockbell can be heard will last like eternal tears.

Dánaíocht

Cé a mbeadh de dhánaíocht ann
A leithéid a dhéanamh
In ainm Dé —

166

Is tú ag moladh rí neimhe agus talún,
Do leabhar a theilgean uaidh
I d'fhianaise i ndomhain Loch nEathach,
Fuar is dubhach, go mbáitear é,
Ansin do lámh a ghlacadh
Agus tú a tharraingt ina dhiaidh
Gan ligean uaidh thar an gcill amach?

Poemfateaudacity

Who on earth would have the poemfateaudacity to do such a thing in the name of God – there's you adjudgepraising the highking of nonskyheaven and drylandsurface-earth, and he soundcondemnthrows your book in witnesspresence before you into the depths of Lough Neagh, rawcold and gloomdark, and it swathsympathybayquenchdrowns, then takes your hand and pulls it behind him without letting go out of the churchyardcell?

Cumhdach

Cé an fear dána a sheasfadh suas
Ag an léachtán sa gcrannóg
In bhur gcill i dTigh Moling
Leis an gCathach a thabhairt
Amach as a chumhdach is ceacht
A thabhairt uaidh
Nó sliocht as Leabhar Chaoimhín
I bhfianaise na mac léinn anois
Is an t-ollamh mór é féin
Ar shlí na fírinne faoi dheoidh?

Guidance-strongholdcherish-shrine

What bold artpoetry man will stand up at the lectern in the crannoghopperframepulpit in your cellchurch in St Mullin's to take the sorrowfulwarlikebattle-reliquarypsalter of St Columba out of its guidance-strongholdcherish-shrine and read a lesson or a posteritytracepassage from the Book of St Kevin in the witnesspresence of the scholars now that the master-poet himself is on the way of last truth at last?

An Tobar Úd Thall

D'éirigh Moling lena chléirigh
Gur chuir gach fear cloch
Ina leacht. *Ionúin é mar leacht,*
Minic a bhí muid beirt
Ag comhrá lena chéile
Seachnóin na conaire.
B'aoibhinn liom é a fheiceáil,
An té sa leacht ar an tobar úd thall.
Is ionúin gach ionad eile
Ina dtaithíodh an té sin Suibhne.

That Well Over By

Moling rose up with his sextonaltar-boyclerics and every manone of them put an islandshorecastletesticlestone from Clogh on his liquidgravestonecairn. *A beloved grave, we used often talk together along the trajectorymountaindogpass. It was sweetdelightful for me to see him, that person in that well over by. And every other haunt of Sweeney's is beloved as well.*

Rody Gorman was born in Dublin in 1961. He has worked as Convenor of the Translation and Linguistic Rights Committee of Scottish PEN and as Specialist Adviser for the Scottish Arts Council. He has published twelve collections of poetry, most recently Beartan Briste/burstbroken judgementshroudloomdeeds *(Cape Breton University Press, 2011). His selected poems in Irish and Scottish Gaelic,* Chernilo, *was published by Coiscéim in 2006. He was recently Writer-in-Residence at the Scottish National College for Gaelic Language and Culture, Sabhal Mòr Ostaig, and lives on the Isle of Skye, Scotland.*

DHÁ DÁNTA

Simon Ó Faoláin

BEDOUIN

Tá an fód cruaidh le sioc ag lóchtaint gréine,
– Beithígh ina staic ag cogaint, gal lasnairde –
Seasann na hardchnoic cúplacha, an Géarán is a Phointe,
(níl na hainmeacha tábhachtach, ná fiú na focail, ach an rud a fheictear)
Fillte i mbrat geal bán, siméadrach, teibíocht as cloigeann Ghréagach
Le huillinneacha caoine rialta ag éirí ar an dá thaobh
Go dtí dígeann an dá bhuaice agus crochta idir
An dá rinn siúd, an drom tanaí ina chuar foirfe:
Corrán diallaite ar chapall cruaidh na cruinne;
Nó bogha athchuartha i ngreim ag laoch Oilimpeach
A bhuaileann súil na sprice le gach iarracht;
Nó bogha Chiúpid os cionn bharra beola méithe
A chuireann tochas ionainn chun a póige.

Ach ní hea, ní hiad, táid na samhail uilig siúd dulta ar fóraíl,
Mar anois is cuimhin liom crot maorga símplí lán mistéire
Ina sheasamh i gcúl dumha gainimh i lár an Sahára,
Uillinneacha arda ar dhá thaobh suas go binn cuaillí
– dhá cheann – is an anairt gheal ag lúbadh síos i mbogha aoibheann
Eatarthu, an oíche tagaithe agus taobh an phubaill aonair
Bhí crógacht tine óir is oráiste ag sméideadh.
Atá sé dóite fós im' chuimhne, ólta inti siar síos,
Mar a bhfaca é trén aer scáinte corcra in am oscailt réalta
Ón 747, ag scrogaireacht muiníl chun cinn ag féachaint
Siar d'fhonn nach dtréigfeadh an radharc mo shúile choíche,
Ach do ghéaraigh ar an uilinn gur éirigh peirspictíocht dodhéanta
Is anois, b'fhéidir nach raibh ann riamh ach sméideadh tine.

TEIFEACH

This is no world for escaped beings
To make their way back into

(R.S. Thomas)

Gur coimhthíoch thú anso ba léir,
Ach nuair a gheitis romham sa ród
Ba chosúil nach mbeadh aon teagmháil
Eadrainn ina eaclóg,
Le báine súile allta ag splancadh
Fé do ghlib rua le huamhan
Roimh an saol seo nó saol eile,
Sciorrais, chasais ag éalú
Ó chiapadh ag an Droichead Bán,
Ag tabhairt bóithrín ort a lúbann
Suas go bearna Mhullach Bhéil
Mar a rinceann aer fiain
Sa tsúil idir grua sléibhe
Agus mala liath néalta:
Duitse, seo tairseach na saoirse,
Lig do ghéim agus osclófar.

Seo mo ghuí duit, a *bò Ghàidhleach*:
Go mbeidh an Féith Fia do d'fholach,
Go dteipe cuardach lucht an *Pet Farm*,
Go dté tú slán le hardchlár Bhréanainn
Mar raon siar go Más an Tiompáin
Is soir go Chathair Chon Raoi uainn,
Ach beir ar dhrom leat ualach éadrom
M'anama i measc na saor.

Simon Ó Faoláin was born in Dublin in 1973 and raised for the most part in Paróiste Mhárthain in West Kerry, where he now lives. He is a professional archaeologist and has written, or co-written, several books and articles on the subject. He holds two degrees from University College Galway. He is the author of two collections of poems, Anam Mhadra *(A Dog's Soul, Coiscéim, 2008) and* As Gaineamh *(From Sand, Coiscéim, 2011).*

DHÁ DÁNTA

Celia de Fréine

From a work in progress, I bhFreagairt ar Rilke/In Response to Rilke.

LYS BLANC

An airíonn sí a dhath de dhath uaithi
de bhrí go bhfuil sí chomh bán sin —

An gcruthaíonn an ganntanas sin loinnir
a chuireann ag soilsiú faoin ghrian í —

An mbíonn sí ag brionglóidí
faoi cé chomh gearr is a bheidh a saol

nach mbeidh deis aici
páirt a ghlacadh i gceiliúradh

go meallfaí chuig a staimín
anáil an adhmholta?

Is féidir liom a piotail a fheiceáil
ag crith faoina mbréaga

a pailín ag greamú dóibh siúd
a cheannaíonn í

ag fágáil a lorg ar a lámha
mar a smeartar *henna* ar an mbrídeach

oíche roimh a bainis
le cur in iúl don domhan
nach bhfuil sí ar fáil níos mó

LYS BLANC

Being so white does she crave
the absence of colour –

does its lack create a radiance
that makes her gleam in sunlight –

does she dream knowing
her life will be so short

that she will not have the chance
to partake in celebration

until the breath of eulogy
is lured towards her stamen?

I can see her petals
shiver beneath their lies

its pollen rub off
on those who purchase her

leave residue on their hands
as henna is smeared on the bride

the night before her wedding
to let the world know
she is no longer available

APRÈS TOUT

Déanann an eala bhalbh ghlórach
sonas a bhronnadh orainn
neamhaird á déanamh aici dínn
nithe eile faoina cúram aici
bia, mar shampla, a hál

Ach is a cumas eitilte is mó
a gcuirimid suim ann —
é chomh grástúil go bhfuilimid
in éad leis an gcréatúr

Dá cheapfaí dúinn an bua céanna
bheadh sé ar ár gcumas againn

Faoi mar atá, sciobann an eala
rún ár n-éada léi
á adhlacadh faoin chré

APRÈS TOUT

The mute glorious swan bestows
happiness on us
even as she ignores us
making other matters her concern
food, for instance, her brood

But it's her ability to fly
that entrances us most —
so graceful
we envy the creature

But were we meant to fly
we would be able to do so

As it is, the swan carries
the secret of our envy with her
burying it in the earth

Celia de Fréine is a poet, playwright, screenwriter and librettist who writes in Irish and English. She has published four collections of poetry: Faoi Chabáistí is Ríonacha *(Cló Iar-Chonnachta, 2001),* Fiacha Fola *(Cló Iar-Chonnachta, 2004),* Scarecrows at Newtownards *(Scotus Press, 2005) and* imram:odyssey *(Arlen House, 2010). In 2009 Arlen House published* Mná Dána, *a collection of her plays, the same year as the Abbey Theatre presented a rehearsed reading of her short play* Casadh, *which it had commissioned.*

DHÁ DÁNTA

Dolores Stewart

AN CHATHAIR
a haithle Cavafy

Adúirt tusa liom: rachainn thar lear
go bhfeice mé cathair eile níos fearr ná an cheann seo.
Nil i ndán dom ar m'urlár féin
ach reilig na mbeo: tá mo chroí i gcré is m'aigne dreoite.
Tré fabhraí na súl, mothaím
fothrach dubh mo shaoil in m' áit dúchais,
agus capaill na blianta ar lár.

A deirim leat: ná chuir turas in aisce ort féin.
I dteach na muintire eile
nil ann ach an seanbhlas céanna, an seanbholadh:
conairt na seansráide ag scamhadh i do dhiaidh.
Agus más drámh é do shaol anseo, is amhlaidh a bheas sé thall,
leagtha amach duit insan craiceann dearg céanna –
ní mó ná mac mioscaise eile.

SEACHRÁN AN RÍ LEAR

Is rí mórga mé go fóill,
cé go bhfuil amadán ó thalamh ag creimeadh mo chroí.

Nach mé an ludramán acu,
iad siúd de mo chuid fola féin a sceith orm?

Nach díol trua mé,
agus aghaidh na dallsíne i mo ghob,

an oiche anuas orm? As béal na gaoithe
ní mó ná tóin na spéire, nil nimh nimhe le fáil

nios measa ná an feannadh a bhfuaireas
as lúb tuathal a lámh. Le chomh glic is a bhíos,

níor mhothaíos sliomadh focal
ag déanamh creille orm agus iadsan i gcrúba an diabhail.

Le barrliobar cogair, guíom anois an dídean
is dual dom fiú as an ngaoth anoir, nó foscadh

as an bhfuacht. Ní rí mar dhea mé,
ach tá amadán ó thalamh ar thaobh na gaoithe orm,

ag cur leaca le mo chluas.

Dolores Stewart is a bilingual poet from the West of Ireland. Her English collections are In Out of the Rain *(1999) and* Presence of Mind *(2005), both from The Dedalus Press. Her Irish volumes, published by Coiscéim, are* Sé Sin le Rá *(2001) and* An Cosán *(2003). She teaches at the National University of Ireland, Galway.*

DÀN

Aonghas MacNeacail

SEUMAS

gu robh thu na do dhuine mór,
do ghuailnean leathann tuathanaich
a' giùlain uallach torrail saoibhreach –
do smuaintean eagnaidh sgaoilte eadar
bòrd is sabhal, muilinn lìn is callaid,
mart is achadh –
          do sgamhan daonnan
a' togail sonais 'o bhi tarraing
          chùbhraidhean an achaidh
gus an sgaoileadh, beò a rithist, thar
dhuilleagan bàna nan leabhar

gu robh thu na do sgoilear, beò eadar
tìm agus tachartas, a stiùir 'nad chùram
do cheòlradh tromh fhead (ro fhaisg)
nan gunna eadar gach lasradh agus
spreadhadh a chlisg an àile ghorm anns
an d'fhuair thu slighe eadar tùs agus gach
tonn is camag ann an cuan doirbh an
dualchais, ann an àraidhean briarach
nan leabhar, ann an
          comhraidhean le
           caraidean is guaillichean

ged a bha caolas eadarain 's nach b' è
an léine creideimh cheudna
          a chòmhdaich ar n' òige,
b'aithne dhuinn luach chnuic,
na bheireadh glac de sheasgair dhuinn,
mar a lean sgeul is searmon na slighean

cama eadar cluas is eanchainn, ach éisd
ri ruitheaman binn nan rann a' dualach
'n an sìomain òrach is iad a' crioslachadh
nan còmhradh eadar sruth is
                    clachaireachd fo dhrochaid,
                        mu bhuanas an t-seirm
gus bann a ghléidheadh eadar léirsinn agus
cuimhne, oir tha 'n ceangal eadar dùthchas
agus gach slighe acrach airson dhàimhean
chlisgeach air fhighe stigh do mhonaidhean
beòtha na h-aigne, agus do nàdar daonnan
airson a bhi streap, feuch dé bha ri fhaicinn
bho na barran
                    agus leis gu'n d'ràinig thu, tha
thu fhéin anise na do bhàrr ameasg nan stùc —
caidil a charaid, seasaidh an leus, gabh tàmh

SEAMUS

that you were a big man
your broad farmer's shoulders
bearing a large fertile burden of riches —
your shrewd thoughts spread between
table and barn, linen mill and hedge,
cow and meadow —
                    your lungs forever
taking delight in drawing
                    meadow fragrances
to scatter them, alive again, across
the blank pages of books

that you were a scholar, alive between
time and occurrence, who cannily steered
your muse through the flute (too close)
sent by guns among all the blazes and
blasts that startled the blue air where

you found a way between source and each
wave and ripple in the tricky ocean of
heritage, in the thorny ladders
of books, in
              conversations with
                  friends and companions

though there was a strait between us, nor
was it the same shirt
              that clothed our youth,
we knew the value of hills,
how much shelter a glade might give us,
how story and sermon followed the wry
routes between ear and brain, but hear
the sweet rhythms of verses plaiting
the golden ropes as they girdle
conversations between streams and
              the masonry under bridges
                about the lasting song
that fastens the bond between insight and
memory, as the knot between origin
and every hungry journey toward skittish
kinships woven into the living mountains
of intellect, which your nature always
wanted to climb, to find what could be seen
from the peaks
              and as you attained that, you
are also to be seen as a peak on that ridge –
sleep friend, the flame will endure, be at rest

Translated, from the Scots Gaelic, by the author.

One of the foremost contemporary poets in the three tongues of Scotland, Aonghas MacNeacail was born in Uig, Isle of Skye, in 1942. He is the author of six collections of poetry, including new and selected poems in Gaelic, Deanamh Gàire ris a Chleoc/Laughing at the Clock *(Polygon, 2012). A pamphlet of poems in Scots,* Ayont the Dyke/Beyond the Wall, *is forthcoming. His songs have been set to music by some of Scotland's leading composers. He now lives in the Scottish Borders.*

A BRIEF CHRONICLE OF MY PRIVILEGE

Pura López Colomé

This captain, my captain ...

My privilege began in 1981, when I heard Seamus Heaney read here in Mexico, a poet whose work I had been introduced to, in the late 1960s, early 1970s, by one of the Benedictine nuns who was my teacher in boarding school in South Dakota. She happened to be Irish, and followed closely, so she said, the poets "from the North."

He was invited to participate in one of the most unforgettable poetry festivals that have ever taken place anywhere, along with a whole pleiad of masters: Tomas Tranströmer, Jorge Luis Borges, Vasko Popa, Octavio Paz, Allen Ginsberg ... We were all sort of mesmerized by the great beatnik, who was supposed to be reading *and* playing some strange instrument on stage. That night I sat next to Tomás Segovia, another luminary, who was very close to young poets of the time, me included, I guess, because his sons were already writing. When he noticed my interest, he whispered in my ear: "Listen. I understand why Ginsberg is so appealing to your generation; but if you are planning to go on translating poetry for that supplement where you work, and you really value music within words, as you say, the guy you should be paying close attention to, the real challenge, is Heaney." He was right.

So, as soon as I got back from Morelia, I started translating some of his poems. Naturally, I found out in no time how difficult it was, much more than anything else I had previously set my mind to. I could not possibly try to publish anything. A couple of years later, when *Station Island* came out, I was so dazzled by it I couldn't resist the temptation to do some translation work. What really stimulated me was Station XI, where the pilgrim gets back home with the "penance" of translating into English some lines written by Juan de la Cruz, one of my very favorite authors. Such a beautiful version by Seamus, *making it new*, sort of speaking to me directly, encouraged me to do the equivalent task, and try to read his poetry as prayers, and then produce an echo in Spanish, *resounding* in my language.

At the time, I used to have a regular space in the literary supplement *Sábado*, published every Saturday as part of the newspaper *Unomásuno*. I started with two of those poems at a time, accompanied by some kind of brief commentary. I gave my private island the title, "Del pantano a la profundidad del aire" ("From Bogland to the Depths of Air"). I didn't know that the man who had invited Seamus to that memorable festival kept sending what I had written to his Harvard address. Several years later, when I was about to finish what I called the first draft of the whole book, by chance I spoke about it with a friend, who happened to be working in the festivals office: "Haven't you ever seen what Heaney had to say about those versions you did?", he asked. How could I have? He then mentioned there was a whole file including his wonderful letters thanking his friend for sending all that material. As I could not have access to those documents, I only asked him to get me Mr Heaney's address in Cambridge. I wrote to him directly, and our correspondence started almost immediately. Hearing from the man himself that he thought the translations were "both daring and right", catapulted me into outer space. I don't want to appear haughty by saying this, but if it sounds that way, please forgive me: I am simply proud. I owe Seamus everything. Here's part of his lesson:

STONE FROM DELPHI

To be carried back to the shrine some dawn
when the sea spreads its far sun-crops to the south
and I make a morning offering again:
that I may escape the miasma of spilled blood,
govern the tongue, fear hybris, fear the god
until he speaks in my untrammelled mouth.

PIEDRA DE DELFOS

Que me lleven a la capilla de madrugada
cuando el mar esparza al sur sus lejanas cosechas de sol,
y yo realice la ofrenda matutina una vez más:
que me salve del miasma de la sangre derramada,
controle la lengua, tema a hybris, tema al dios
hasta que se exprese sin trabas por mi boca.

If anything was aiming at language, at the danger of overstepping the mark, and moving south, precisely in my direction, it was this, just like Auden's line speaking of poetry making nothing happen, and then carefully adding: "it flows south, from ranches of isolation and the busy griefs, / raw towns that we believe and die in; / it survives, a way of happening, a mouth."

This Mexican mouth was receiving some tacit validation, I thought. When *Station Island* was almost ready, we spent a sabbatical year in Seattle, Washington, thanks to my husband's academic activity. That Christmas, when my father-in-law asked me what I wanted as a gift, I knew I wanted an airplane ticket for the following spring, to go meet Seamus in person in Pennsylvania, where he was supposed to be reading and lecturing. I crossed the US. After going through a bit of the translations, he simply wished me luck. As soon as the book came out, thanks to the wonderful attitude of the artist Francisco Toledo, who was not only the editor, but even designed the cover, I sent *Isla de las Estaciones* to Seamus's Dublin address. He wrote me one of the most beautiful letters I have ever received. Not long after that, I received through the mail a copy of *Seeing Things*. How could I get such a gift without feeling I was meant to render it into Spanish?

This is the early 1990s. This is the busier and busier Seamus. This is the period previous to the Nobel Prize. Nevertheless, he never stopped answering my letters and faxes, being as helpful as possible without actually intervening in my work. He mostly let me swim on my own. A couple of years after the Nobel Prize, in 1997, the recently appointed Mexican Ambassador, Daniel Dultzin, invited me to come to Ireland for the first time. This was quality time. I attended Cúirt, heard Seamus reading, had many conversations, Jamesons and cigars with him. The year after that my version of *Seeing Things* was published by Conaculta in Mexico under the title *Viendo visiones*. I went to San Francisco to give it to him personally. He was happy enough with the "sound of those twelve-liners." It was there and then he said he would consider accepting the invitation to come to Mexico again. And he did.

So far, the books had been published only in Spanish – there wasn't a bilingual edition yet. When I knew for sure he was coming, I got in touch with the Dutch artist Jan Hendrix, who had done a fantastic book with Seamus's translation of the *Aeneid*. He was very enthusiastic about doing something else with him, and this was a perfect opportunity for it. After being asked, Seamus sent me ten poems related to poets and poetry, which made the first bilingual publication coming my way. As it turned out, it was trilingual: English, Spanish, and Dutch, with beautiful screenprints done by Jan Hendrix. The book was called *The Light of the Leaves / La luz de las hojas*.

Seamus visited Mexico once more for this special occasion, gave readings in both Mexico City and Oaxaca. I translated three of his essays, published in a limited edition, given as a commemorating gift to all those who attended the main reading. I couldn't believe what was happening; I didn't know how to deal with this privilege. The only thing I could do was to go on, and on, and on.

Therefore, right after this, I went on with *The Spirit Level* (*El nivel*), insisting on bilingual editions from then on. This one was launched at the Mexican Embassy in Dublin in the year 2000. That night, somehow the conversation took us to Glanmore, his sonnets, and to sonnets in general. Seamus asked me if I had ever written one. When I said no, he replied: "You should try it – it's really the only way to experience the tug of both the ship and the anchor." I did start to follow his advice, though not in my own poetry but in his, and very little by little, over many years, for we both decided to include all the sonnets scattered in all his books. In between came the selected essays from *Finders Keepers*, entitled *Al buen entendedor* in Mexico.

Because he was frail during those years, I didn't bother him much with queries. He did remind me at some point, though, of what he had said to me years before, when he realized how committed I was. "Don't forget I was born to be translated into Dutch", the untranslatable being inside the music of the language that produced the work. Dutch is near Anglo-Saxon, in other words, nearer to Seamus, and my language, in that respect, close to Latin. So, I decided to do a double version of each sonnet: first, a rhythmically freer one as a point of departure from which I did another one, more faithful to the form of the sonnet in Spanish. Before he saw the final product, I did send him copies of the photographs by Alberto Darszon to be included. Finally, the collection was ready for his seventieth birthday. I thought he would live forever.

The translation of his last book, *Human Chain* (*Cadena humana*) went without saying. I did go to Dublin to launch it with him in a bilingual reading. As if all this was not fortune enough, Seamus decided, there and then, to read some of my poems in English translation. The voice that had been with me for decades has been since then recorded in my hard disk, my heart.

Just some months before he passed away, Trinity College asked Seamus to inaugurate its newly born Literary Translation Center, for which ceremony a special reading was organized. They asked me to choose some of my favorite poems in translation for a publication designed to commemorate the occasion. I chose, among others, the first and last poems of *Cadena humana* for two different reasons. The first one refers to (finders keepers) that specific moment in which an occurrence is put on your way, your life, for you to increase your attention, a sort of Aleph, the oneness of God, as well as Borges's point in space that contains all other points. In other words, poetry incarnate, in whose atmosphere plurality of each word, each line, each stanza, is never questioned: one thing is all things.

HAD I NOT BEEN AWAKE

Had I not been awake I would have missed it,
A wind that rose and whirled until the roof
Pattered with quick leaves off the sycamore

And got me up, the whole of me a-patter,
Alive and ticking like an electric fence:
Had I not been awake I would have missed it,

It came and went so unexpectedly
And almost it seemed dangerously,
Returning like an animal to the house,

A courier blast that there and then
Lapsed ordinary. But not ever
After. And not now.

DE NO HABER ESTADO DESPIERTO

De no haber estado despierto, me lo habría perdido:
El viento se alzó y giró, haciendo resonar al techo
Entre las hojas del sicomoro al vuelo,

Y me levantó en un resonar idéntico,
Vivo y pulsando, un alambrado eléctrico:
De no haber estado despierto, me lo habría perdido:

Llegó y se fue inesperadamente
Y diríase casi peligrosamente,
Como un animal camino a casa,

Una ráfaga mensajera en fuga,
Pasó como si nada. Para nunca
Jamás volver. Y ahora menos.

So this was my moment containing all moments: had I not been awake, I would have missed it. And the last poem symbolizes to a certain extent the act of translation, being as it is, Seamus's translation of a poem by Pascoli. And it is about a kite. Taking the opportunity of the English version's use of both kite and comet, this was my chance to use *cometa*, the Spanish word, as well as *papalote*, the Mexican Spanish word, originating in the Náhuatl for butterfly. The heart being a kite for me, this comet that includes my dear language, as well as my feelings and emotions, I cannot feel but grateful for everything this captain did, whose heart gave meaning to my own creative forces. Here's just the last part of the poem:

A KITE FOR AIBHÍN

[...]
And now it hovers, tugs, veers, dives askew,
Lifts itself, goes with the wind until
It rises to loud cheers from us below.

Rises, and my hand is like a spindle
Unspooling, the kite a thin-stemmed flower
Climbing and carrying, carrying farther, higher

The longing in the breast and planted feet
And gazing face and heart of the kite flier
Until string breaks and – separate, elate –

The kite takes off, itself alone, a windfall.

UN PAPALOTE PARA AIBHÍN

[...]
Y ahora revolotea, jala, se desvía, se clava de soslayo,
Se levanta, se deja llevar por el viento, y de inmediato
Se alza ante nuestros gritos jubilosos desde abajo.

Se alza, y mi mano es un huso que se va desovillando,
El papalote una flor de tallo delgado trepando
Y llevando, llevando más lejos y más alto

El anhelo en el pecho y los pies plantados
Y el rostro que contempla, el corazón de quien el papalote
Vuela hasta que – separada, exaltada – la cuerda se rompe

Y el papalote despega, por sí solo, como caído del cielo.

And from here, I take off on the wings of Heaney's blackbird, paying tribute forever to the man and his work, to this captain, my captain, who will be missed with every heartbeat, with every wing-flap.

One of Mexico's most distinguished poets and translators, Pura López Colomé was born in Mexico City in 1952, but also spent part of her childhood and youth in Mérida, capital of the state of Yucatán. When she was 12, following her mother's death, she was sent to a Catholic boarding school run by the Benedictine Sisters in South Dakota. Of this American period she has written, "The Sister who taught English was Irish: I owe her my early enthusiasm and later devotion to poetry in general, as well as to Irish poetry in particular. It was there I wrote my first poems, and translated, perhaps a bit too boldly, some poetry by W.B. Yeats and Patrick Kavanagh." On her return to Mexico after high-school graduation, she took a degree in Spanish and Latin American Literature at the Universidad Nacional Autónoma de México. She is the author of nine books of poems, most recently Santo y seña *(Watchword, 2008), and* Reliquia *(Relic, 2009), and selections of her poetry have been translated into English by the American poet Forrest Gander (*No Shelter, *Graywolf Press, 2002). She is also the celebrated translator of five books of Heaney's poetry, including* Sonetos *(Heaney's Sonnets, 2008), and* Cadena humana *(Human Chain, 2011), both published by DGE Equilibrista.*

HEANEY HELIOS

Askold Melnyczuk

We were here once.

Writing poetry may be a way of breathing underwater for its maker but the paradox is that in the process the tank is never depleted. It fills, and stays full no matter how many draw on it. While the air can, in some cases, feel heavy, Heaney's verse is laced with helium, its buoyancy a matter not only of sonic frisson but of a subversive visionary gleam. That, at least, is the quality I find in the volume I return to most often these days, *Seeing Things*. Its perfectly framed narratives seem to repose in the elusive equilibrium of earned wisdom:

> I love hushed air. I trust contrariness.
> Years and years go past and I do not move
> For I see that when one man casts, the other gathers
> And then *vice versa*, without changing sides.

The zen of this reminds me Heaney came into his own in the sixties and that he spent the pivotal year of 1970–1 teaching at Berkeley. He himself acknowledged he was politicized by what he saw, finding in the self-assertion of African, native and Latino American liberation movements encouragement for Ireland's own struggles. The awareness honed an edge. He sounded a contemporary note inside classical meters scored in a diction so richly infused by the landscape and weather of rural Éire as to constitute its own language. If you're not careful, you might trip on quernstones or blunder into a Mossbawn bog, or even tumble down a corbelled tomb, losing your pampooties on the way, deep in the geography of the commonplace. Not even a glossary to Heaneyish guarantees a certain keying to the map.

Sometimes the only way to master the terrain is by imposing on the gregarious cartographer himself – one adept at finding those lost portals by which pilgrims may traverse both distance and time. Fortified by lunching on the "split bulb and philandering sigh of ocean", the travelers paid respects before the Flaggy Shore, Martello Tower, Maud Gonne's grave, and in our famous group photograph. (*Editor's Note: A photograph of Alexandra Johnson, Ellen Driscoll, Tom Sleigh, Lynn Focht, Seamus Heaney, Sven Birkerts — Heaney's "Cambridge-area friends". See page 51.*) The place: Coole Park (swans barely visible in the left-hand corner). The weather: gray, wet — a "soft day" the Irish call it. The mirroring lake returns to the sky the nothing it gives. But nothing is needed because "Whatever is given / can always be reimagined." We were here once. And here we remain.

Askold Melnyczuk is the Director of the Creative Writing Program at the University of Massachusetts Boston. He is the author of three novels, Ambassador of the Dead *(Counerpoint, 2001),* The House of Widows *(Graywolf, 2008) and* Smedley's Secret Guide to World Literature *(forthcoming). He was a friend of Seamus Heaney.*

PLACE-PAINT

Murdo Macdonald

Near allied.

I first saw someone who looked very like Seamus Heaney walking down the paved street in Stromness in Orkney during the St Magnus Festival of 1994. Later the same man turned up at a lecture I was giving in the Pier Arts Centre. It was indeed Seamus. My talk was on themes in Scottish art and one of the images I showed was of a work by William Johnstone, a very abstract landscape in which the only real hint of the land itself lies in an implied horizon. It's a beautiful work and I tried to explain that it was a work deeply concerned with the nature of place and also with the nature of painting itself. Not that I really had to, because the image spoke for itself. But at the end Seamus made a comment: "I liked what you were saying about that artist's place-paint." And of course that is what I'd been trying to say: "place-paint" – whether the meaning that one takes from the phrase is the painting of place or the placing of paint.

Some years later, in 2003, I had the good fortune to give the address for Seamus when he accepted an honorary degree from the University of Dundee. Two things remain with me about that day: first was Seamus's keen hope that there would be a pipe band – and, being Dundee, of course there was. Second was his description of Sorley MacLean's poetry as evoking "the political and the visionary … near allied", a phrase that I adopted in my address to describe Seamus himself. But however many honours were bestowed on Seamus, for me he will always be the poet who sat at the back of my lecture and came up with the beautiful notion of "place-paint".

Murdo Macdonald is Professor of Scottish Art at the University of Dundee. He is the author of Scottish Art in the Thames & Hudson World of Art series, and was Editor of The Edinburgh Review *from 1990 to 1994. He was one of the three Scottish Editors for* The Other Tongues: An Introduction to Writing in Irish, Scots Gaelic and Scots in Ulster and Scotland *(Irish Pages, 2013).*

COLONEL SEAMUS

Don Bogen

From Berkeley to Cincinnati ... and beyond.

"Go for it — savagely" was what Seamus Heaney advised me a day before I flew out to be interviewed for a position at the University of Cincinnati. We ran into each other in the Men's Department of J.C. Penney in Berkeley in spring of 1976. I was looking for a necktie conservative enough for a job interview (well, any necktie, actually — it was 1976), and Seamus was thinking about gifts to bring back from his second stint as a visiting professor at the University of California, the one he undertook without Marie and the children. This is the visit recalled in "The Skunk", one of his finest love poems — for him, absence truly did make the heart grow fonder that spring. Seamus and I had met at a party at the home of my dissertation director Josephine Miles, whose bent for the democratic contrasted sharply with the hierarchical nature of the Berkeley English Department in those years. To celebrate Seamus's return, Jo invited not only faculty poets, but also postgraduates like me, undergraduate poets, community poets — anyone with an interest in the art.

Thanks to Seamus's advice and some good fortune, I got the job and started work as an assistant professor in fall of 1976. Among my more pleasurable duties was to select visiting writers in our series of readings and talks, so, one evening in February 1979, my wife Cathryn and I found ourselves heading to the Cincinnati airport, which, as travelers are often surprised to hear, is actually across the Ohio River in Kentucky, normally a 20-minute drive in good traffic. But we ended up going through a blizzard, our drafty Volkswagen bus barely able to snake its way up the long hill from the river, both shoulders of the freeway littered with cars that had spun out and given up. We got there — but only after two nerve-frazzling hours behind the wheel. I stumbled through the airport's sliding doors with my eyeballs feeling as if someone had been pummeling them and my hands shaking.

Seamus's plane had arrived — on time, as it turned out — but he was not to be found at the arrival gate or baggage claim. Where else to look? The bar, of course, and as we approached I saw him coming forward with a snifter of brandy in each hand: the poet as St Bernard, ready to revive those nearly defeated by winter's blasts. Noting the context here, I should say that I'm not referring to the actual saint but to the dog that bears his name. I have to admit too that, though Seamus's patience and warmth of welcome met the highest of canine standards, Cathryn and I always thought he resembled a sheep more than a dog – it must have been that blur of hair: dark in those days, pure white a few years later.

By the time the three of us had finished our brandy (Seamus had left his at the bar), the roads were clear. We made it home, and what followed was a three-day house visit that turned out to be full of memories. Some of these were not the happiest – I think about making our slow, damp way uphill on uncleared sidewalks the next day, trying to convince Seamus that this kind of snowfall was not normal for southern Ohio – but they are all rich. I remember his reference to the Danish archeologist P. V. Glob as he introduced the bog poems: the way he savored not just the wit of the name but its sound and feel in the mouth. "Glob" – now that's a Heaney word if ever there was one. I remember the best conversation I ever had about poetic technique as we discussed Yeats's use of alternate-rhymed iambic trimeter on our way to a restaurant – I think of this every time I teach "Casualty". And I remember the three of us sitting around the narrow fireplace in our apartment, with bourbon this time, talking about literature – not so much discussing as celebrating and, yes, performing it, as when Seamus recited the opening of *A Portrait of the Artist as a Young Man* from memory. I suppose I should say the four of us, as our daughter must have caught the rhythms of both the writing and the laughter from her position *in utero*.

Anna was born two months later. As I write she's about to turn 35. She's a scholar, of early twentieth-century fiction actually – so perhaps Seamus's recitation had some effects. Seamus and my wife Cathryn both left this world in 2013. After teaching Seamus's books, mostly *North* and *Field Work*, a dozen times each and working with some 30 doctoral students on their own books of poetry over the years, I find myself a professor emeritus this spring. (*Emeritus* – I can imagine how Seamus would rib me about that. And I'd deserve it for insisting on addressing him as "Colonel Seamus" after he'd received that particular distinction from the University of Kentucky, just an hour or so south of here, across that river again.)

Though I was eager to be employed back in 1976, it's hard to believe I've ever gone for anything "savagely." But I have repeated Seamus's advice when my own students have left for job interviews, and it pleases me to think that some of them may pass it on to their students in Atlanta and Green Bay and Hattiesburg, Mississippi. I'm not sure I can manage to have brandy (or the equivalent) at hand for a weary host when I fly somewhere for a reading, but I hold it as a model of visiting-poet generosity. And I hold Seamus as a model visitor, friend and companion in the art. Like many, I owe him considerably more than a brandy.

Don Bogen is the author of four books of poetry, most recently An Algebra *(University of Chicago Press, 2009). His poems have appeared in* The Paris Review, The Yale Review, Ploughshares, Stand *and other journals. In 2011 he was a Fulbright Distinguished Scholar in CreativeWriting at the Seamus Heaney Centre for Poetry at Queen's University Belfast. He is Nathaniel Ropes Professor of English and Comparative Literature at the University of Cincinnati and serves as poetry editor of* The Cincinnati Review.

a boarder

Donal McLaughlin

Work-in-progress.

Died there, aye. I heard it on Radio Foyle, God have mercy on him. Sad, isn't it? Seamus Heaney, dead. He'd not been well apparently but.

Our Liam, God rest him, went to school wi him, ye know. Aye, sure the priest came up to my mother and father's door specially thon time even. Pleaded wi them to let Liam stay on at the school & go to St Columb's. "He's got what it takes alright, Mr & Mrs O'Donnell. A very intelligent boy you have there. Very able. A sin against God it would be not to, not to let him continue." Some new reform there was. Had just been introduced. So they didn't have to pay nothing & aye, let him. Stead of putting him out to work.

A day-boy Liam was. Not a boarder. Fact he'd done so well in his Qualifying but meant he hadn't to pay for his books, or anything like that there. Heaney – wi being from *County* Derry, not Derry itself – was one of the boarders. From Toomebridge he was, right? Or Castledawson. Liam anyhow was given special permission to go back in at night. To do his exercises lik. He wouldn't've had a hope in hell in the house sure, wi the umpteen of us round him. Pandemonium it always was – as ye can imagine.

To cut a long story short anyway: the boarders sometimes would've got Liam to bring them fish 'n' chips in, to stop at the fish 'n' chip shop on his way. That – if you're wondering – is how he first met Seamus Heaney. Oh aye, the boarders got fed an' all alright. Sometimes but, they'd've taken the notion for a bit of fish or a chip. Our Liam wouldn't've been able to afford any himself, of course. Some of the boarders but would've given him share. I know for a fact young Heaney did. A couple of chips, say. A corner off the end of the fish. To taste his mouth lik.

Did ye never hear that one? It's true enough, ye know. God knows, he'd no shortage of stories, Liam, from them years. Time he was caught smoking, for instance, by the president him-buckin-self. Or the weeboy Feeley who fell out of a tree onto the railings – an' here one went up his arse. "Rectum", – the story goes – the master tried to call it. "Wrecked him?" another weeboy reporting it said. "It nearly bloody killed him!" Four of the cane, thon "bloody" & thon "arse" cost him. Two on each palm. Naw, it doesn't, does it, say much for the masters. The stories Liam would tell ye rarely did. They could be bad brutes at times, right enough, the Christian Brothers. Forty-eight of the cane, our Liam got one time. Monsignor what's-his-name it was, not that he was a monsignor at that point. Six was the maximum, supposed to be. *Eight* times but, Liam was given six – of the *best* – in that-there lesson. The last one of the day. He'd been caned in every single class before that too. Every single master had hauled him out & laid buckin into him. Heaney, whoever seen him, lik all the other youngfellas, had to watch.

Okay, aye, so he'd stayed away from school for six months, Liam. That doesn't make it right but. He never ever forgave the monsignor. For years after that sure, any time his photo turned up in the *Journal*, our Maureen – to rub it in lik – would've cut it out & made sure Liam seen it. She posted it over to Scotland forgodsake too sure – for the sheer bloody devilment just. Long dead, Monsignor would've been & she'd Liam, God rest him, cursing like a trooper still.

Heaney will've had his fair share of the cane an' all, no doubt.

The Brothers will've seen to that –

That's not what I was wanting to tell ye but. Naw, fast-forward forty years, more maybe even, an' it was some craic seemingly over in Paisley one night. Liam & Bridget were long over in Scotland by this stage, the weans had flown the nest all probably even, the older ones for sure. Young Liam, their eldest, would've been thirty, say, *at least* already – judging by the age of some of his cousins. The same one anyhow ended up hearing Seamus Heaney one Saturday. At something-or-other he went to, up at Clydeside Uni. Heaney apparently was one of the four speakers & got up & read a poem that wasn't even finished. Magine! Being invited over & reading them all a poem that wasn't even done yet! Ye could understand it maybe if he'd started to give them a *song* – only, in the middle of it, to blank on the words. Bad enough, that would be. To be invited over to Scotland but, then stand up & announce ye were going to read them something that wasn't even done yet – well, I'd want my money back, me! No one blinked an eye but apparently. Our Liam swore that his Liam swore: no one as much as batted a buckin eyelid. Naw, it was Big Liam, more lik, who lost the rag nearly when he heard what the poem was about. The subject of it, ye see, was a class at St Columb's all them years ago. An English class. Seems the master – Gallagher, his name was – always made the boys read out a book. What d'ye call him-there again, him that wrote all the plays? Shakespeare, aye. Aye, an' whichever of all them plays it was, they'd to read it in class lik, weren't allowed to take it home wi them, so the master would get the youngfellas each to read a part out. Every time a new character entered or opened his mouth to speak finally, someone was told to be him. Young Liam was gobsmacked seemingly, found it hard to believe that was how it was done back then an' all. In the forties or fifties in Derry, I mean. *He*'d been subjected to the exact same thing in the seventies, ye see. In Paisley but. Dia-buckin-bolical, it had been. Heaney's poem – bit he'd actually written anyhow – was powerful but. Powerful altogether. It nearly made ye glad even, ye'd to suffer lik that at school.

What it was, ye see – he said – was: Heaney didn't just tell ye the names of all the weeboys, tell ye who was asked to read each part. Naw, the thing about Heaney was: he toul ye an' all whose weeboy it was, what his da done for a living. What part of Derry they were from an' all maybe. He'd mention some youngfella having green socks on. Or a turn in his eye. Being fond of a good spud. Another would've had his finger up his nose when the master decided to call on him. Young Liam had lapped all this up, seemingly. He'd never raved about a poem in his life, he said. Was raving about this one but. Genius it was – giving ye that particular take on it all.

In full stream he was seemingly when all of a sudden he just shut up lik. Clocked the buckin look his da was giving him. "What's wrong wi your face?" he asked, a bit taken aback. It wasn't lik him, wasn't lik him at all lik, turns out but, our Liam was worried. Worried Famous Seamus – as some people came to call him – had mentioned him an' all lik. Don't laugh: Prospero O' buckin Donnell. Going to sue him he was, he said, take him to the bloody cleaners he would if that-there poem ever, ever, as much as buckin mentioned him. *In progress*, his arse. "I doubt you've much to worry about, da", his son Liam interrupted him. "An' anyhow, there's no guarantee the guy'll ever publish it. Fact, there's no guarantee he'll even finish it. You could be worrying for nothing." Seems he bought a book specially, Liam, to get it signed & toul the man himself his da had gone to school wi him. Not, right enough, that Seamus minded him lik. Naw, the name Liam O'Donnell meant nothing to him.

That, needless to say, set our Liam off again. "Is that all the gratitude I get for smuggling their chips in? He knew my buckin name at the time alright. The rest of them all an' all! They knew it alright when they were wanting something!"

"That's buckin boarders for you", he hissed. "Haven't I always bloody said so?"

"Catch yourself on, da", young Liam seemingly said to that. "Forty-odd years have passed. You can't expect —"

That but wasn't how his da buckin seen it.

Not at that point anyhow.

Even if he did come round.

Editor's Note: In both collections of short stories by Donal McLaughlin, there is a loose sequence of "Liam stories" that move between Derry and Paisley, in Scotland. In the above story, the Heaney poem "discussed" by Liam Senior and Liam Junior is "The Real Names", from Electric Light *(Faber, 2001), which records Heaney's schoolmates in various classroom recitations of Shakespeare — one of whom, in fact, is named "Liam McLelland".*

Donal McLaughlin was born in Derry in 1961, but moved to Scotland in 1970. He is the author of two short-story collections: an allergic reaction to national anthems *(Argyll Publishing, 2009) and* beheading the virgin mary & other stories *(Dalkey Archive, 2014). He was Scottish PEN's first* écrivain sans frontières, *and is featured in* Best European Fiction 2012 *(Dalkey Archive). His translations include work from over 100 German-Swiss writers for the* New Swiss Writing *anthologies (2008–2011). He continues to live in Scotland.*

THAT HAND & OTHER INTERLUDES

—

Tom Mac Intyre

Never faltered.

—

THAT HAND

We have this saying where I come from – "May the giving hand never falter."
Reminds me of Heaney every time I hear it. Seamus had the giving hand.
Never – over half a life time of livin' on tin clippin's – did I know it to falter.
The talk is, say, of the concert about to be performed. His hand wanders to
your breast pocket. Invisibly, so it seems. He winks, the hand withdraws.
You fumble thanks. "Took me a long day", he told me once, "to learn the
simple act of giving." Pause. "Always let me know when need is at the door."
"Thank you, Seamus" – I said it often. Taught me a lot, he did. Giving. Rest
easy, *a mhic.* Knife on the stone – "A giving hand that never faltered."

—

THE SONG OF THE YELLOW HAMMER
for Muireann

is widely known as
"little-bit-of-bread-and-no-cheese" –
that was enough for me

the summery Saturday morning
I made for the remotest
corner of our five acres –
bushes, rushes, heedless stream,
timber galore, fir mostly,

got lost on the way, lost
again soon as I got there,
three times lost on the dander
home, saw and heard

what I'd come for, take
my word, yellowhammer
and I met eye to eye –
nobody blinked, it was a
greeting like no other,

as I do live and sigh,
the yellowhammer's call,
I can confirm, "*little-bit-of-
bread-and-no-cheese*", this

was all of seventy (or so)
years ago, wasn't that long
out of High Infants but
knew what I should be
chasing summery Saturday
mornings ...

———

Now and again, as the fit
dictates, I'll warble to my
grandchildren – "*Little-bit-
of-bread-and-no-cheese*",

recite them my walk in
the wilds Saturday morning
epic, age of innocence,
that enamoured dawning,
two in ten will attend,

fair enough hit, don't
you fancy, the times, Christ,
that's in it, I promise
this pair a joint ex-
cursion, as quickly can-

cel the voucher – "It's a solo,
truly, trip", I amend patiently, "it's discovery, it's
swoon, immersion, re-
creation, it's *being* under

seven of a Saturday
morning, your education –
sans chalk or blackboard –
begun, song of the yellowhammer, countless other
gifts, yours forever, thrown

you for your diversion
or, say, ritual immersion,
but let's not, Holy, Holy Smoke,
solemnise the dance, enough
pulpiteers loose as is,

that's it for today, *mes amis*,
now sing after me, please –
'*little-bit-of-bread-and-no-cheese*'" –
and, girl, do they comply!

THE GOLDCREST

Most have never seen
the goldcrest. And for why?
Because gold is the
price you pay.

Most people never forget
their one sight
of the goldcrest.
And for why?

Because gold, gold,
gold, gold, gold,
is the price you pay.

EXIT
for Dermot

This morning word of his demise.
Last time we met, a few months
ago, dowdy café, Boondocks County,
you could tell, look at those eyes,
nobody home, no, nary a one.

We talked Mick and Pat, Kate, Mary,
the priest's housekeeper, parson's pup.
Volubly driven, the pair of us
nailed together an *Interlude*. Title?
"Spiel about anything, bar Death."

There was the odd pause, in which
you could hear the piper slowly,
aye, and fife lowly, that was okay,
we stuck at it, gave our best.

Did he seem afraid? Tricky call
that. All right, say, say *hunted*,
haunted. More the former, for sure
the former. Say this: never saw
him more stripped. Scaresome.
Love him you could. True fact.

Tell you one thing, and I'll say
Slán abhaile. Was Granny told
me. "Departure Lounge is where
it's at. Truth of it. Dewfall.
While people bake bread. Brew tay."

THAT DAY
for C

Let there be beautiful women
there aplenty, you in the van.

Spring day, please, lick o'rain
now and again, only dry rain.

Incessant gabble. Story-tellin'. Lifelong seanachie going under. "Any
good?" "Fit for little else", I heard
one of the sons there remark –
meanin' no harm now, no knife.
Played in goal for Cavan, it's
written that writers keep goal. Look
at Paddy Kavanagh, Albert Camus,
if you don't mind, others we
might mention. "Why – wait a
minute – do writers play in goal?"
"Participation, non-participation,
got it?" "Gotcha." He could spell – on
the good days – the forward's intention, position himself. Pray ..."

"Was he any damn use?" "Had
his moments. Give him that now,
yon game in Irvinstown, Jesus,
Christ Almighty … Shiver ye …"

"Where do they come from?" "Who?"
"Scribblers." "No tellin. Alarmed, they
take up the quill, scratch till
they drop. Not the full shilling,
I believe." "That it?" "Close to it."
"Not a bad oul' day." "Saw worse …"

*A poet, dramatist and fiction writer in both English and Irish, Tom Mac Intyre was born in
Cavan in 1931. He is the author of eight collections of poetry, most recently* Stories of the
Wandering Moon *(The Lilliput Press, 2000),* ABC *(New Island Books, 2006) and*
Encountering Zoe: New and Selected Poetry *(New Island Books, 2010). His plays for
The Abbey Theatre include* The Great Hunger *(1983),* Good Evening, Mr Collins
(1997) and his version of Brian Merriman's Cúirt An Mhean Oíche/The Midnight
Court *(1999). A collection of short fiction,* The Word for Yes: New and Selected
Stories, *was published by the Gallery Press in 1991. He is a member of Aosdána, and lives
in Lurganboy, Co Cavan.*

THE ROCK OF HOREB

Exodus 17:1–7

Andrew Philip

Who sets the hard-set to such weeping
they can slake the thirst, can quench
the quarrel burning in a wandering folk?
I am no instrument. What rings
from the struck rock is not
what was wrung from me.
I am no aquifer. Nothing of
life whispered through my fissures
till that single blow pushed me
to bow to a fresh and giddy spring.
I couldn't quell its pressure, couldn't
name the force that split me
open like a loaf just risen
from the oven's grave; split me
clean open like a pomegranate,
the juice I didn't know I held
bleeding into gaping, grateful mouths.

Andrew Philip was born in Aberdeen in 1975 and grew up near Falkirk. His first full collection of poetry, dealing with bereavement, The Ambulance Box *(Salt, 2009), was shortlisted for the Aldeburgh First Collection Prize and the Seamus Heaney Prize for Poetry. His second collection,* The North End of the Possible, *was published by Salt in 2013. He now lives in Linlithgow, and is one of the two Scots Language Editors of this journal.*

FILE NA FLAITHIÚLACHTA & TEANGA AN GHLEANNA

Cathal Ó Searcaigh

FILE NA FLAITHIÚLACHTA

Ag meá na bhfocal.

Nuair a bheannaigh sé duit, an mheidhir shéimh úd ina shúile, an miongháire sochmaidh úd ar a bhéal, bhraith tú go raibh sé do do bheannú.

Agus bhí.

Shamhlaigh mé riamh naofacht leis agus beannaíocht. Chan é gur cráifeachán a bhí ann. Chan naofacht chúng, cheartchreidmheach de chineál ar bith atá á mhaíomh agam ach rud inteacht níos bunúsaí, níos leithne, níos daonna.

Uaisleacht anama agus grástúlacht aigne.

Agus é ag caint leat bhraith tú go raibh a umhail ort, go raibh a intinn leagtha ar a raibh le rá aige leat — cé gur iomaí rud eile a bhí aige le bheith ag smaoineamh air — go raibh sé ag déanamh cúraim duit.

D'éist sé leat. Thug sé uchtach duit asat féin. Bhronn sé tíolacthaí a dhaonnachta ort.

Ba chuma cé thú féin, nuair a dhírigh Séamus a sholas ort bhí tú sa ghlóir.

Duine tar an choitiantacht a bhí ann. Thabharfá faoi deara i gcruinniú nó ar an tsráid é. Bhí sonraíocht air, tarraingteacht as an ghnáth ann agus é de bhua aige daoine a ghairm chuige. An cineál céanna aoibhe air a bhí ar Nelson Mandela nó atá ar an Dalaí Láma.

Ar ndóigh, bhí sé ina Rí ar a ghairm féin, ach níor chuala éinne é ag déanamh gaisce as a cháil féin.

Duine modhúil a bhí ann nach raibh dúil ar bith aige an solas a bheith air ach ní raibh dul thairis aige. Chuaigh a gháir i bhfad agus i bhfairsingeacht. Rinneadh gairdeas roimhe cá bith áit ina raibh sé, sa bhaile agus i gcéin.

Cé go raibh sé ard i gcéim agus i gcáilíocht ní raibh ardnós nó éirí in arde ar bith ag gabháil leis. Chleacht sé an tsimplíocht. Sheas sé leis an choitiantacht.

I gcomhrá sháraigh sé i gcónaí an focal achrannach, an focal nimhneach, an focal cointinneach.

Rinne sé a sheacht ndícheall snáithe réidh na cainte a aimsiú agus coinneáil ar an díreach.

Ní fhacthas riamh go raibh naimhdeas, goimh nó binb ag baint leis. D'éirigh sé os a gcionn le daonnacht agus lena dhearfacht.

Ní duine é a rinne achrann a ghéarú nó a luigh isteach ar ghearradh cainte. Ní raibh an domlas nó an drochrún ina dhúchas. Agus dá dhonacht iad lucht a cháinte, choinnigh Séamus guaim ar a theangaidh agus ní thug sé de shásamh daofa a bheith gearánach.

Ina áit sin ghair sé a bheannacht leo. Ba sin an sórt a bhí ann. Mórchroíoch agus fadcheannach.

Fear é a bhí i dtólamh ar lorg an tsochair do dhaoine eile. Rinne sé rudaí ní chun a thairbhe féin ach chun leas na coitiantachta. Níor chleacht sé a beith buntáisteach.

Níl inse béil ar an obair a rinne sé ag cuidiú agus ag tacú le daoine; an focal sólásach a thug dóchas duit sa dorchadas, an focal moltach ar ócáid cheiliúrtha, an focal comhairleach i gcluais ar uair na guaise.

Rinne Séamus comharsanacht mhaith lena chomhfhilí, dream a dtig leo a bheith niogóideach go maith. Dá chomhartha air sin an meas a bhí air i measc na suadh, ní amháin ar leac an dorais aige féin in Éirinn ach ar fud an domhain mhóir.

Ba doiligh leis éinne a dhiúltú agus dá dhroim sin, bhí sé i gcónaí faoi bhrú oibre; léamha, léachtaí, ócáidí áitiúla, ócáidí stáit, cruinnithe, comhdhálacha.

Chuirfeadh a chuid dualgaisí poiblí duine ar bith thar a fhulaingt ach lean sé leis á thabhairt féin go fial.

Is minic a chuir sé é féin thar a acmhainn le duine nó dream éigin a shásamh, mar nach raibh sé ann dul siar ar a fhocal.

Thug sé an dúthracht sin leis as a óige. Mac feirmeora, bhí an dícheall agus an dualgas sin leis ina dhúchas. Ní raibh cnámh leisciúil, ní raibh féith fhalsa ina chorp.

Chrom sé ar a chuid oibre, chuir sé fuinneamh lena ghuth agus thug sé a shaol ag fónamh ar mhaithe leis an fhilíocht.

Ba deas i gcónaí a shiúl réidh, coiscéim scaoilte an tsaothraí talún. Níor chaill sé riamh a ghreim sa talamh, ná a dháimh le bunadh na tuaithe. Ba iadsan a chré. Ba iad an chuisle bheo, bhríomhar, bhisiúil a choinnigh brí ina shamhlaíocht agus seasmhacht ina dhearcadh.

Bhí Séamus dílis dá dhúchas, dá thógáil, ach ní raibh sé teanntaithe taobh istigh de theorainneacha treibhe.

Labhair sé linn as fairsingeacht aigne níos leithne ná an treibh, as doimhneacht tuigbheála níos buaine ná ár ndomhan beag duthain.

Ar nós Yeats, ar nós Rilke, labhair sé linn as an eagna dhomhanda.

Ba léir go raibh file mór tagtha ar an bhfód nuair a d'fhoilsigh sé a chéad chnuasach, *Death of a Naturalist*, i 1966. Chuir sé lena ghealltanas sa tsaothar a tháinig uaidh go rialta thar na blianta. Cnuasach ar chnuasach ag cur lena chéile is ag méadú a reime is a chéime mar phríomhéigeas an Bhéarla. Gach ceann acu saothraithe i gceárta an tsaoi agus múnlaithe ar inneoin an tsaoir.

Ach anois, tá gabha geal an dáin imithe uainn. Is mór an trua nach bhfuair sé spás beag eile den tsaol ach tháinig an uair agus an ócáid in aicearracht.

Tá muid faoi smúit anois. Tá file an chroí mhóir ar shiúl uainn.

Dá mba ghá focal a rá ar ócáid shollúnta nó ag imeacht suáilceach, ba é Séamus ba ghrinne a labhair. Agus cé nach bhfuil smid as a bhéal inniu, labhrann a dhánta linn agus labharfaidh go brách.

Agus is fiú a mheabhrú gur saolaíodh Séamus cúpla mí tar éis bhás Yeats i 1939. I gcasadh cinniúnach na beatha tig muid agus imíonn muid. Tá rotha mór an tsaoil ár gcasadh de shíor ó bhroinn go bás is ó bhás go hathfhás. Ní thig aon ní a chur ar ceal. Maireann a raibh ann, a bhfuil ann agus a mbeidh ann. Tá na mairbh á mbeathú i mbroinn na mbeo.

———

POET OF AMPLITUDE

Weighing his words.

When he greeted you, the gentle mirth in his eyes, the placid smile on his mouth, you felt he was blessing you.

And he was.

I always associated him with sanctity and piety. It's not that he was a pietistic person. I'm not suggesting any kind of narrow, orthodox piety but something more basic, broader, more human.

Nobility of soul and graciousness of mind.

As he spoke to you you felt that you had his attention, that his mind was fixed on what he had to say to you – although he had many other things to think about – that he was taking care of you.

He listened to you. He gave you faith in yourself. He bestowed on you the gifts of his humanity.

It didn't matter who you were, when Seamus directed his light on you, you were exalted.

He was someone out of the ordinary. You'd notice him in a crowd or on the street. He was remarkable, with an extraordinary attractiveness and the ability to call people to him. He had the same pleasant expression as Nelson Mandela had or the Dalai Lama has.

Of course, he was king of his own calling, but no one ever heard him boasting of his own fame.

He was a modest man who never wanted the limelight but couldn't avoid it. He was heard of far and wide. He was acclaimed wherever he was, at home and abroad.

Although he was of high degree and fame he had no formality or airs about him. He practised simplicity. He stood with the common people.

In conversation he always overcame the quarrelsome word, the venomous word, the contentious word.

He did his very best to find the smooth thread of the talk and to stay on the straight path.

He was never seen to have any hostility, sting or venom. He rose above them with humanity and with his positiveness.

He wasn't a person who aggravated a quarrel or practised castigation. Gall or evil intention were not in his nature. And no matter how bad his critics were, Seamus held his tongue and didn't give them the satisfaction of complaining.

Instead he called his blessing to them. That's how he was. Big-hearted and long-headed.

He was a man who always sought good for other people. He did things not for his own benefit but for the good of the commonality. He was never advantageous.

There's no describing the work he did helping and supporting people; the comforting word that gave you hope in the darkness, the word of praise on the occasion of celebration, the word of advice in the ear on the hour of danger.

Seamus built a good relationship with his fellow poets, people who can be quite testy. An indication of that is the respect he had among the sages, not only on his own threshold in Ireland but throughout the wide world.

He found it hard to refuse anyone and, consequently, he was always under pressure of work; readings, lectures, local events, state events, meetings, conferences.

His duties would overstrain anybody but he continued on giving himself generously.

He often overstrained himself to satisfy some person or group, because it wasn't in him to go back on his word.

He brought that devotion with him from his youth. Son of a farmer, that diligence and duty were in his nature. There wasn't a reluctant bone, there wasn't a lazy vein in his body.

He bent to his work, he put vigour into his voice and he gave his life in service for the sake of poetry.

Always pleasant was his easy walk, the free stride of the tiller of soil. He never lost his grip in the land, nor his fellow-feeling for country people. They were his clay. They were the vital, lively, productive pulse that kept life in his imagination and constancy in his outlook.

Seamus was faithful to his nature, to his upbringing, but he wasn't fixed inside tribal parameters.

He spoke to us from breadth of intellect broader than the tribe, from deep understanding more enduring than our transient little world.

Like Yeats, like Rilke, he spoke to us from worldly wisdom.

It was obvious that a great poet had come on the sod when he published his first collection, *Death of a Naturalist,* in 1966. He abided by his promise in the work he produced over the years. Collection after collection in conjunction, enhancing his authority and his status as master poet of the English language. Every one of them cultivated in the sage's smithy and shaped on the anvil of the mason.

But now, the silversmith of the poem has gone from us. It's a great pity that he didn't get another slice of life but the hour and the occasion came soon.

We are despondent now. The poet of the great heart has gone from us.

If a word was to be said on a solemn occasion or at a joyous event, Seamus was the most discerning speaker. And although there's no sound from his mouth today, his poems speak to us and will speak forever.

And it's worth remembering that Seamus was born a few months after the death of Yeats in 1939. In the fateful twist of life we come and we go away. The big wheel of life is forever turning us from womb to death and from death to aftergrass. Nothing can be extinguished. All that was, that is and that will be, lives. The dead are being nurtured in the womb of the living.

Translated, from the Irish, by Seán Mac Aindreasa.

———

ó TEANGA AN GHLEANNA

2

"Cuir an fód íochtar in uachtar
is músclófar an pór
atá ina chodladh faoi thalamh",
a déarfadh sé i dtólamh
agus é ag oibriú i gcré a chuimhne
le scéal ón tseanré
nó nath éigin cainte
a thabhairt i gcraoibh
le haoibh a chur ormsa.

Bhí mé ró-óg le leas
a bhaint as an tseanchas
a bhí i dtaiscidh i gcréafóig
thorthúil a chuimhne
nó le meas a bheith agam
ar úire thalún a aigne
is nuair a cuireadh é
thug sé leis chun na cré
fómhar feasa a dhúchais.

Anois seo mé ag gabháil
i gcosúlacht leis
lá i ndiaidh lae is mé

ag tiontú na créafóige
i m'iomaire beag féin
de theangaidh na treibhe;
ag iarraidh a bheag nó a mhór,
an pór atá i bhfolach
in ithir na bhfocal
a bhíogadh chun craoibhe.

3

Is é is cúis mo chaointe anois
go bhfuiltear ag ligean
do ghabháltais na teanga
is d'ithir mhéith an dúchais
a ghabháil chun fiantais
i bhfearainn bharr an Ghleanna.

Tá talamh tíre mo mhuintire
á thréigean, an míntíriú is an saothrú
a rinne siad i gcuibhrinn úra
na saíochta, an leasú i ngoirt
na líofachta, an síolchur fada
i gcréafóig mhín na cainte ag gabháil
faoi scraith gharbh an dearmaid
i gcúig achadh seo mo chineáil
i bhfearainn thréigthe an Ghleanna.

Is é cúis mo chaointe anois
go bhfuil an t-aos óg dá dtógáil
ar díth a ndúchais is a dteanga;
dream bocht stoite gan bhród
ag éirí aníos ar thalamh tur an easbhaidh
ina nglúin gan fód
i bhfearainn loma an Ghleanna.

4

Inniu tá an seanbhunadh ina luí
i leapacha na n-éag
is tá teangaidh eile i réim
san áit a raibh buanaíocht ag a ngéaga
le cuimhne na seacht nduine.
Anois tá a dtailte amuigh bán
is a n-éifeacht chainte gan iomrá.
Níor shamhlaigh siad ariamh
go dtiocfadh an lá
nach mbeadh a dteangaidh
faoi ghrásta na buanseasmhachta
anseo i Mín a' Leá.

Is a ndálta siúd ní rófhada
go mbeidh do ghleosa is d'iomrá
imithe as cuimhne na mbeo
is an píosa beag talaimh seo
a shaothraigh tú mar fhile
imithe i bhfiaile na faille.
Bí i do thost feasta, a chroí.
Tá tú i bhfeascair do lae.
Rachaidh tú i gcré
in ithir mhilis do mhuintire
sa talamh dílis a dtáinig siad i dtír air
in am na díthe, in am an anáis.

Beidh anam sa chuideachta
is tú ag meascadh leis an tseandream;
fir chnámhacha an tseanchais
is mná géagscaoilte na scéal.
Gaolta líofa na gcnámh!
Brollach le hucht, giall le leiceann,
bhur lámha thar a chéile,
dhéanfadh sibh bhur gcomhrá
go fada buan i suan na gile
sa teangaidh a chan bhur ndaoine

ó thánadar thar droim na díleann
le Míl is lena mhac, an file.

8

Tchím í go fóill, caor dhearg an chaorthainn i mbláth
a leicinn agus in ainneoin go raibh sí anonn i mblianta
bhí sí ógánta ina cuma. Seanbhean dhiaganta a chan
glóire Dé is a Shoiscéal. "Níor lagaigh sé ariamh mo ghuth",
a déarfadh sí. "Go dté mo bheatha i mbláth is i mbiseach Dó."

Tchím í m'aigne, drúcht glé na maidine ag dealramh chugam
as a ceannaithe beannaithe, as a caint dhiaga.
"Is tú cré d'athara agus paidir do máthara'" a deir sí go ceansa
agus muid ag comhrá cois bóthair. "Tá tú ag fáilt tógáil mhaith."
Éistim léithe, a cuid Gaeilge chomh súmhar le sméara na gcraobh.

Tchím í sa tsiúl, seál dubh casta ar a cloigeann
maidin Domhnaigh agus í ag pilleadh ón Aifreann.
"Ní bheidh i bhfad go dtiocfaidh na haingle fá mo choinne",
a deir sí go dáimhiúil, brú anála uirthi ag tógáil na malacha.
"Níl siad i bhfad ó láimh anois le cuidiú Dé."

Seo anois mé is an saol ag teacht géar orm féin
is gan aon rómhuinín agam i nDia righin an tSoiscéil.
Shéan mé a ghnása, sháraigh mé a bhéasa, ghéill mé
do Dhéithe na nDúl; dóibh siúd ar umhlaigh mo chineál
roimh theacht do Chríost. Ach a Chiot, a dhuine dhil,

níor thréig mé an teangaidh dhiaga, an teangaidh phágánta
a bhí i mbláth a toraidh i do chuid cainte agus cé
go bhfuil sí ag meath san áit a raibh sí líofa, craobhach le do ré,
is díthe a thugaim mo dhílseacht, díthe a shléachtaim glúin.
Do theangaidh, a Chiot; béal na bé agus urlabhra mo Dhéithe.

from THE GLEN'S TONGUE

2

"Bring the bottom sod to the top
and you'll waken the seed
that is sleeping underground",
he used to always say
as he worked the soil of his memory
to bring an ancient story
or some verbal gem or other
out into blossom
to make me smile.

I was too young to be nurtured
by the lore stored in the cultivated
loam of his memory
or to realise the fruitfulness
of his fertile mind
and when he was buried
he carried with him into the clay
the stored wisdom of his *dúchas*.

Now here I am turning
into his likeness
day after day
while I turn the soil
in my own small furrow
of the dialect of my people;
striving more or less
to waken towards fruition
the seed of words
hidden in the tilth.

3

I am in mourning now
because the smallholdings of language
and the rich earth of *dúchas*
are being let run wild
in the townlands at the top of the Glen.

The tilled land of my people
is being abandoned, while their taming of it,
their labour in the new haggards
of erudition, their fertilisation
of fluent meadows, their long sowing
in the fine tilth of conversation
are fading below the rough forgotten sod
in these five wide fields of my kindred
in the deserted townlands of the Glen.

I am in mourning now
because the young are being raised
dispossessed, bereft of language;
a rootless remnant without pride
surviving on the infertile ground of loss
a generation without soil
in the bare townlands of the Glen.

4

Today the old ones rest
in their eternal beds
and a new language has tenure
where their limbs had been settled
for as long as the townland remembered.
Now their land lies fallow
and no longer noted for their eloquence.
They could never have foreseen
the dawning of the day
their language would no longer

hold graceful enduring sway
here in Mín a' Leá.

And as with them it won't take long
for your voice and your name
to leave the memory of the living
and for this small holding
you cultivated as a poet
to be left to weeds and to wildness.
Hold your tongue from now, dear heart.
Evening has come upon your day.
You will go into the clay
into the sweet earth of your people
into the loyal soil that helped them hold course
in the time of need, the time of want.

There will be life in the company
when you mingle with the old crowd;
the bony men of lore
the loose-limbed women of stories.
The eloquent kinship of bones!
Breast to bosom, cheek to jaw,
your arms twined together,
you will converse together
and forever in that splendid restfulness
in the language used by your people
since they crested the flooding wave
with the bardic son of Míl.

8

I see her still, the scarlet of rowanberries flowering
in her cheeks and she had, although she was getting on,
a young look about her. A pious old woman who sang
the glory of God and Gospel. "May my voice not falter",
she'd say. "Until I blossom and bloom again in Him."

I see her in the mind's eye, a gleam like morning dew
haloing her features, illuminating her sacred speech.
"Your father speaks through you, and your mother prays", she says kindly
as we chat at the side of the road. "You're being well nurtured."
I absorb her words, her Gaelic succulent as berries on the branch.

I see her walking, a black shawl wound around her head
on a Sunday morning returning from Mass.
"It won't be long before the angels come for me",
she says genially, breathless from the rising slopes.
"They're within easy reach now with the help of God."

So here's me now and the world grown threatening
and me with no great faith in the rigid God of the Evangelists.
I renounced his rites, transgressed against his customs, gave fealty
to the Gods of Creation; to those to whom my people bowed
before Christ came to be. But Kitty, dearest Kitty,

I did not abandon the divine tongue, the pagan tongue
that flowered and fruited in your speech, and though it may be
that it withers now where it blossomed rampantly in your day,
it is to it I pledge allegiance, to it I bend my knee.
Your tongue, Kitty, the utterance of the muse and the speech of my Gods.

Translated, from the Irish, by Paddy Bushe.

LABHRAIM LE LÍ PÓ

Tá mé san aois sin anois,
ré na seanaoise
go dtig liom mo chomhrá
a dhéanamh leatsa, a mhian,
tar dhuibheagán na gcianta.

Mé i mo shuí ag ól fíona
amuigh faoin spéir
oíche shoiléir i dtús an fhómhair —
do leabhar os mo chomhair —
Tá fios i bhfíon, a deir tú,

agus mé ag baint sú as úll
órbhuí na gealaí
atá ag teacht i gcraobh
ansiúd ar bharr an Eargail.
Cruthaíonn fíon a fhilíocht féin,

mar is eol duitse, a chroí,
a d'imigh le hól is le ceol.
Drabhlás diaga na hÉigse!
Ar an tslí sin scaoil tú saor d'aigne
ó ghlais is ó gheimhle an tsaoil.

Sílim a mhór duit,
a fhir lán de mheidhir,
a fhánaí na ndán, a fháidh an dúshláin,
a bhris gach gnás is nár fhan dílis
ach amháin do chúram an dáin.

Ba mhaith liom a mhaíomh
go bhfuil cuisle ghaoil againn
le chéile agus muid beirt ag ceiliúradh
an tsaoil seo nach bhfuil seasamh ann.
Saol na trioblóide! Saol na brionglóide!

Bhí tú beo i dtréimhse doiligh,
dreamanna ag troid fá chríocha,
cogadh agus creach ar fud na Ríochta.
Chuir tusa do dhóchas i ndánta,
mo dhálta féin, le tú a thabhairt slán.

Is chuaigh tú le fán an tsaoil,
ag triall le scamail shiúlacha
thar sléibhte is thar aibhneacha,
ag ligean liúnna áthais leis na géanna fiáine
is ag comhrá go gáifeach leis an ghealach.

Anocht is mé bogtha le fíon
cluinim Abhainn Bhuí na filíochta
ag sní idir dhá bhruach an leathanaigh.
Siúd tú faoi sholas na gealaí.
Le mo dhán, beannaím duit

thar an duibheagán.

SPEAKING TO LI BAI

I'm of that age now,
those declining years,
that I can converse
with you, precious one,
across the abyss of the years.

I'm sipping wine, sitting
out under the stars
on a crisp, early autumn night –
your book spread before me.
In vino veritas, you observe,

as I take joy in the juice of the golden
yellow apple of the moon
that is filling towards ripeness
over there on the summit of Errigal.
Wine ferments its own verse,

as you yourself know, dear heart,
who gave yourself to drinking and music.
The divine dissipation of Art!
And so you freed your mind
from the world's fetters and fastenings.

I think the world of you,
you most convivial of *viveurs*,
vagrant versifier, oracle of opposition,
who burst through custom, whose only loyalty
was to the business of poetry.

I want to assert
our pulse in common
when both of us celebrate
this world that does not abide.
Here's a world of trouble! A world of dreams!

You lived in interesting times,
ethnic wars, border wars,
conflict and destruction throughout the Kingdom.
You placed your trust in poetry,
as I did, for your salvation.

And you wandered through your world
travelling with restless clouds
over mountains and rivers,
sending joyful screeches to the wild geese
and having lunatic conversations with the moon.

Tonight, airy with wine,
I hear the Yellow River of poetry
flowing between the banks of the page.
There you go in the moonlight.
With my poem, I send you salutations

across the abyss.

Translated, from the Irish, by Paddy Bushe.

Cathal Ó Searcaigh is the Irish Language Editor of this journal. He was born in 1956 and raised in Meenala, near Gortahork, an Irish-speaking district in Co Donegal. His poetry collections are Súile Shuibhne *(Coiscéim, 1983),* Suibhne *(Coiscéim, 1987), the bilingual* An Bealach 'na Bhaile / Homecoming *(Cló Iar-Chonnachta, 1993),* Ag Tnúth Leis an tSolas *(Cló Iar-Chonnachta, 1993),* Na Buachaillí Bána *(Cló Iar-Chonnachta, 1996), the selected* Out in the Open *(Cló Iar-Chonnachta, 2000),* Gúrú i gCluídíní *(2006),* An tAm Marfach ina Mairimid *(2011), and* Aimsir Ársa *(2013). His prose works include* Seal i Neipeal *(2004),* Light on Distant Hills: A Memoir *(2009), and* Pianó Mhín na bPreáchán *(2011). He is also the author several plays in Irish, and a selection of English translations of his poetry,* By the Hearth at Mín a' Leá *(Arc), appeared in 2005. He continues to live in Meenala, and is a member of Aosdána.*

REMEMBERING THE MAESTRO

Chris Agee

Bereavements.

Poor Nano

not much
of a worker
a bit
of a fuck-up
what with
the drugs
yet it was he
who planted the tomato-patch
giving it
halfhearted attention
like so much
in life
where later
early one august morn
I would take
a photo
of Miriam
holding her bowl of tomatoes
that even still
holds her still life
on the hall wall
above
the vanished scene

On the terrace
Žrnovo, Croatia
August 2012

Heaney's death

suggests to me
beguilingly
wisely
here on Miriam's bench
that a small life too
can finish
whole and rounded
even if
for both lives
the might-have-been
might have
been
still more
finished
round and whole

Above Žrnovo
September 2014

A space

but not a place
was promised
in a dream
that ran all night
in fitful images
of waiting
un-*claritas*
where no name
or time came
till
at the old five o'clock wake-up hour
of slow-burn pain
the rooster's republic
again clarified
uncovenanted surplus
of a Congo square
living free
"a dividend
from ourselves"
at the crowing dawn
and the blue sandbar
moon
that awaits
outwith

i.m. *S.J.H.*

Poem begun in sleep
Žrnovo house
September 2014

These whispering poems

snail-tracks
in the sun
dwelling for a time on gravel
an unravelling
skein of travelling
consciousness
friable as its earthed
lightening

Morning road
Žrnovo
September 2014

Author's Note: The last two micropoems above make allusion to phrases in two Heaney poems, "On His Work in the English Language" and "Postscript". All four are taken from a series of 180 micropoems, entitled "Real Realities".

Chris Agee is the Editor of this journal. His third collection of poems, Next to Nothing *(Salt, 2009), was shortlisted for the 2010 Ted Hughes Award for New Work in Poetry, funded by the Poet Laureate and organized by the Poetry Society in London. He is currently working on a fourth collection, and divides his time between Belfast and Glasgow, where he is the Keith Wright Literary Fellow (Writer-in-residence) at the University of Strathclyde.*